What people are saying about

Soulp

T0168471

This is a beautifully written   ic
experience of a spiritual journey. Reading these pages was like
a warm homecoming celebration; a coming home to self. The
writing and content speak to the spiritual novice and more
seasoned traveler, as well. It's a book written with love to teach
us how to love ourselves, as souls on the path and as female.
There are many exercises to assist in the journey and Alessandra
shares her insights and experiences in a very personal way. I am
so pleased to bear witness to this wonderful offering of love to
the world.
Bernadette Pleasant, the Emotional Institute

Alessandra's work is heart-centered immersion into the deepest
experience of being. It calls you into the depths of intuitive insight
where you can discover the ecstasy of communion with life itself.
Kim Chestney, author, *Radical Intuition: A Revolutionary Guide to
Using Your Inner Power*

Soulphoria by Alessandra Sagredo is a book unlike any other.
It is music to the soul; a soothing balm to the fretful mind. To
date I have been on my spiritual path for ten years. I have read
countless books about spirituality and assumed this would be
like many others which I have encountered. Needless to say, I
was very wrong! Alessandra's words are so deeply moving they
are almost like poetry. Each one conjures up vivid imagery and
helps you connect deeply to the messages within the book.
Alessandra has managed to write a book for both beginner and
advanced spiritual practitioner alike. It takes the reader through
each practice in a cohesive manner, which is wonderful for those
who are new to the spiritual journey. But, alongside this, there is

a whole new way of connecting to both Spirit and the soul that other books have not touched upon. A deeper, more practical manner that allows the reader to develop a strong relationship to Source but also to themselves.

Alessandra helps us to understand ourselves – body, mind and soul. Each practice is a tangible and hands-on way to nurture this relationship. I absolutely loved *Soulphoria* and I feel it's a book that should be on everyone's bookshelf. It's one that I will turn to time and time again to help me continue to develop my spiritual journey.

Katie Oman, author, *Self-Love Pledge*

This book is a call to embody as you – the true, powerful, sensual, wise you. Rather than just thinking about it, Alessandra invites you to feel it, play with it, and experience it. Have you always longed to have a life that expresses who you really are more fully? Read *Soulphoria*.

Jacob Nordby, author, *The Creative Cure*

A practical guide to exploring and anchoring the eternal light of the soul, *Soulphoria* offers readers easy, useful exercises to explore the beauty, treasure and power of divine wisdom through easily accessible means. The author's heart-centered poetry is an additional inspiring resource to this book of radiant self-love.

Carole J. Obley, author, *Wisdom from the Spirit World*

This is a book that'll guide you back to your most powerful self, all while showing you how to lean into and receive support from your body, mind, soul, and of course, the earth and universe. You'll feel free and empowered after reading this book, more easily able to guide yourself back into your center and feel the peace that this brings.

Cassie Mendoza-Jones, bestselling author of *You Are Enough*

Soulphoria

A Provocative and Practical Approach to Spirituality

Soulphoria

A Provocative and Practical Approach to Spirituality

Alessandra Sagredo

BOOKS

Winchester, UK
Washington, USA

JOHN HUNT PUBLISHING

First published by O-Books, 2022
O-Books is an imprint of John Hunt Publishing Ltd., 3 East St., Alresford,
Hampshire SO24 9EE, UK
office@jhpbooks.com
www.johnhuntpublishing.com
www.o-books.com

For distributor details and how to order please visit the 'Ordering' section on our website.

Text copyright: Alessandra Sagredo 2021

ISBN: 978 1 78904 882 7
978 1 78904 883 4 (ebook)
Library of Congress Control Number: 2021933228

A CIP catalogue record for this book is available from the British Library.

Design: Stuart Davies

UK: Printed and bound by CPI Group (UK) Ltd, Croydon, CR0 4YY
Printed in North America by CPI GPS partners

We operate a distinctive and ethical publishing philosophy in all areas of our business, from our global network of authors to production and worldwide distribution.

Contents

Dedication

To Armand. The man who has made it possible for all my dreams to come true. With our love anything is possible.

A rhythm exists in each of us, a vibration which when understood allows us to smoothly, sensually and prosperously dance our way through life.

We may be "Spirits having a human experience," but then let's embrace this experience our essential selves have chosen for this life; let's not neglect it.

Let's utilize the Ocean of Knowledge that is available to us (Intuitive Insight).

Let's embrace our incredible innate gifts (Feminine Magick).

Let's begin to become Creators of this reality, instead of passive beings.

Let's live fully, sensually, colorfully, passionately and abundantly proudly moving through this world.

Let's form a love affair with life, one that brings both our internal Spirit and external Human Self a life we savor and love. One we will never forget!

Introduction

What is Soulphoria?

Imagine an orgasm, the blood pumping, sensations heightened, the explosion, where you feel as if you're holding heaven within your grasp. Now multiply this threefold – a fire roaring throughout your entire system, until it burns forth and leaves a beautiful spiraling mark on the world around you. This is Soulphoria. A sensation that brings forth exhilaration, vivaciousness, and fulfillment. The feeling of perfection in the now.

Soulphoria is that moment when your entire spiritual and physical makeup are aligned. It can happen during meditation, on the dance floor, rolling under the covers with a lover or simply going for a walk.

During Soulphoria the channel of energy that flows from your Spirit is unhindered. To reach this state of fulfilled bliss requires that you open the channels of mind, body, and soul. Each one forms a bridge for the energy of your Spirit to fly forth like a phoenix and burn brightly in the present moment. It's simple, yet complex. It's a web of divine bliss, of heat, that sears through you yet doesn't burn, but instead fuels your love of life.

Meet Your (Semi) Human Guide

Although as a child you would often find me tea-partying with entities (who I came to understand, only I could see), the tidal waves of past life recollections began in my 30s and have continued to surprise me to the present day.

I was raised in a very conservative Christian home, both parents being Ministers (Salvation Army officers).

My parents used to say that I danced before I could walk. Being in near constant motion and in a house where dancing wasn't always "acceptable," I turned to spinning. It filled me with pure childlike freedom and glee.

The first spiritual experience (I can recall) was in my bedroom in Saskatoon, turning around and around in circles. I was spinning in my room when I collapsed on the ground next to my bed. I can still remember seeing my toys lined up in my closet in front of me as if my Cabbage Patch dolls were eyeing me wondering, "What is she doing?!"

I recall now that as I spun, I also believed it was a gateway to escape this planet and be in my full power, if only for that moment. My memories of spinning include the thoughts, "If I can just go faster... I can leave... and cross over to be with the beings who love me, so I could experience them as physical entities."

The room was then full of spirits; beings which were half-man, half-bird surrounded me. I recall instantly realizing that my parents were pushing their lifestyle on to me based on the god they believed in. And I realized they were wrong, but not to worry as the Universe didn't care. It was an incredible feeling that settled into me and since has set me free from the need to be right about my beliefs or to convince anyone else of what they should believe. Although I didn't fully understand what was happening at the time.

As an adult, I was able to put it all into context through spiritual exploration and study. That's what really inspired me to write this book, to reach out to others with similar experiences and help them find an authentic path.

From that point forward, I've always been curious and open to anything beyond this reality. However, it wasn't until I reached my early 20s that I had my next nudging forward experience.

This particular spiritual shift point was during a work event, where a very well-traveled, educated and insightful colleague and I were out for drinks. I can remember her reaching across the plush chairs and grabbing my hands and saying, "There's something you don't see in yourself, something special about you. You are meant to do more than your marketing work." Her energy embraced me with a warmth and sincerity. I can remember chills went through me as something deep inside me awakened to what she said. After that I began to seek out anything that could open me up. When I returned to Vancouver, I made my first visit to Banyan Books – a spiritual and metaphysical bookstore – seeking out anything that would provide tangible exercises to help me step into whatever I was. I was on a hunt to garner my own power.

A few months later, my ex met a man who would soon become one of my spiritual conduits. First, they became friends, and one of their conversations turned to the mystic realm. It was at this point that my ex mentioned me and my infatuation with mysticism. So, they set up a meeting between his teacher (whom we will call Bill) and myself.

I remember the day I first met Bill. It was a clear day (which is unusual for the gray rainy city of Vancouver), and as I started to climb the stairs to his apartment in the West End, my body began to buzz. When I reached his door, it felt like the top of my head burst open and energy surged up my spine. As he opened the door and greeted me, it was like returning home to an old friend. I had never experienced this before.

We quickly became very close, and spent a lot of platonic, yet intimate, time together. It was with Bill that I had my first past life regression and soon began to practice using my seeing abilities. My first regression took me to a place outside of this planet, as well as on-planet. The amazing aspect was, Bill could see what I could see. I can remember him hugging me during one of our sessions in the ethereal realm and my body responding with a sigh in the physical realm. It taught me the power of what is possible and reinforced my belief in the fact that we are so much more than what we experience in this reality. And we can trust our visions and insights.

From that point forward my life has been blessed with numerous events like the above. And, of course, many challenges as well in every key area of life (from love to finances and health). Each of these have taught me the valuable lesson that just because you're tapped in and spiritual, doesn't mean you're protected from bad things or else you wouldn't be living the life you were meant to live. Bad things can and do happen to good people, and one of my goals for this book is to help make you stronger when facing life's challenges.

The cosmos had brushed up against me, teasing me into listening, flaunting its knowledge like a seductress filled with wisdom. Insight. Knowing. Guidance.

Awakening Again – My Big C Experience

I don't recall the day I found out I had cancer, I think the trauma was so intense that I blanked out, lost all memory. It's amazing what you experience when you discover you have a walnut-sized tumor growing in your brain.

I recall thinking, "Was I in a car accident? Did someone hit me?", but it was just my body rebelling. And now, over a year later, I look back and can finally say I understand. Although I'm grateful for the changes this traumatic experience has brought, I would never ever want to go through this again.

This book was born from the power of personal resilience.

Born to a teenage black mother who was forced to give me up for adoption with a specific proviso that the adoptive parents were ministers, my journey began. Growing up in a strictly religious household of Salvation Army officers, I was taught that we are worthless sinners before I could read or write. Discovering my bisexuality in my teens I closeted my feelings, knowing too well the consequences of my coming out.

And yet I persisted. I had an early, unhappy marriage which culminated in a divorce in my late 20s.

This was a rough period with financial bankruptcy and

the loss of custody of my only child. And yet I still smiled and soldiered on. I had to start all over again reinventing and rediscovering myself.

But life, it seems, was not quite done with testing my resilience.

Two months after my 41st birthday, my doctor's MRI discovered a walnut-sized, as it turned out inoperable, brain cancer tumor.

The trauma of the initial shock left me with a memory loss surrounding the first few weeks post-diagnosis. I chose to fight. And use everything I knew. I pulled on every ounce of my personal power, every shred of genuine support both from this dimension of reality and from others. Eventually after months of hospitalization, seven rounds of various chemotherapy cocktails, and a lot of intense personal intention and magic, I managed to win over that threat as well. Using many of the techniques I will share with you in this book.

At every point, I could have crumbled and lost myself like many of the people I witnessed in the oncology ward. But instead, I kept going, mostly with a smile on my face, my head held high and unwavering faith in myself.

I have willfully chosen over and over to not be a victim, but to use every experience to help me become healthier and stronger every day and every way!

Resilience is key to living a long, wonderful life. Ready for any challenge.

I hope that your journey to Soulphoria, things I apply daily and everything I've learned will help you find your source of resilient energy and a life of bliss. I am living, breathing, walking proof that it works!

Honestly, this whole book was born from the power of personal resilience.

A Message from My Soul to My Mind:
I won't lie to you and tell you this will be an easy experience, but it will be life changing. This is something you can't force. It's going to take time for you to heal and move past this stage and potentially much longer to heal the scar residue and remnants. But I know that you're strong, fierce, and courageous enough to beat this. That you have the strength and the willpower to go beyond this roadblock in life.

Simply put, my big C Experience was terrifying. I had so many ups and downs, of trusting and then burying myself deep inside of the shadows within me to hide from everything including the light. But a few things helped me get through this.

When you're going through changes and challenges whether emotional or physical (or just in general), consider these:

1) Surround yourself not only with people who love you, but also people who believe in you. They must believe in the power you have to heal, the strength you have to fight this and your own resolve to win this.

2) Don't blame yourself. This is not your fault.

3) Be willing to accept professional help. There are situations in life where we need to lean on another. Don't be embarrassed or ashamed to accept assistance.

4) Stay active and social. You may want to hide from the world, but that won't help you get through this. Slipping into your own precious state of depression, anxiety, or fear, listening to your own bad talk (or negative inner voice) can destroy your sanity. By keeping your activities and social relationships alive, you will help yourself feel normal and move through the process with a deeper sense of well-being.

5) Realize that food is a nourishment. Everything you put into your body can impact you – helping or hindering it – so by

seeing what you eat as natural medicine you will become more aware of what will help fuel your body.

6) Decide and relax into the fact that it's going to be okay – garner the inner conviction of a positive outcome.

Although I would never want to experience cancer again, I can say that I now understand why I went through what I went through. I've changed on a cellular and energetic level. Not only has my physical state become a priority (which I now know how to love and care for like I would a small child), but also my emotions have opened up. I'm more fluid and flowing, and life has become more vibrant. I've fallen in love with the textures of life. Plus, it has redirected me back to my path of writing and sharing myself with the world around me.

You can move through challenges while recalibrating your sense of self and connecting with benevolent spirits that will help you. Let my energy embrace yours. You'll see how amazingly strong you are.

You may also reveal to yourself that you are meant to be here, that the world wants you here and that there is beauty in your power.

Navigating this Journey Together

I'll be your enthusiastic guide, taking you through the 6 points of initiation from

1) Flirtation of the Cosmos: Where you will begin to recognize the nudging, whisperings, and occasional shoves that your ancestors, guides, and spiritual support teams have been helping you with.

2) Embodying the Soul: Heal your relationship with your body and prepare it for Soulphoria.

3) Spiritual Striptease: Where you will strip off false layers.

4) The Sublimely Naked Soul: You will learn how to move

confidently in your authentic self.

5) Becoming a Mistress of Mysticism: Here you heal your relationship with the feminine and tap into your own magic.

6) Then our final stop is the realm of Soulphoria!

Each part of the journey includes exercises to help you apply the learnings to life. You'll find a reference to each related exercise at the end of each relevant chapter. From there, you can decide to explore the exercises right away or after finishing the part of the book.

Tips To Help You Get the Most From Your Journey

1) Treat it like a mini meditative vacation.
   a. Try this: Take the time to set yourself up comfortably somewhere you can be (mostly) undisturbed.
      i. Now hold your hands up in front of you and look at your left hand, into it you place your past.
      ii. Now take a deep breath and look at your right hand, into it you place your future.
      iii. Now bring your hands together in prayer position and breathe into the moment.
      iv. Now you're ready to dive in!
2) Take your time reading each part.
   a. Allow it to absorb into you.
   b. Each part of the book starts with a mini-invocation – it's a great idea to start by reading the invocation and sitting with it while it opens up hidden aspects of yourself.
   c. Don't rush.
3) When exploring the mystic moments, understand these are channeling and journeys. There may be terms and linguistics you're unfamiliar with, however, I've done my best to add a glossary at the end to provide an explanatory note.

4) When doing the exercises – try them for a week at a time.
5) If you have the time and patience – read each part a week at a time then do the exercises.

The Embarkation

"A bird doesn't sing because it has an answer, it sings because it has a song." — Maya Angelou

I have a song, but it does not belong to me alone. When I pitch in with my own harmony it may be unique to me, but the song belongs to many of us. It belongs to the ancient and the new. The young and the old.

This is the song we sing together. The one we long to dance to, to lose ourselves in, to celebrate life under the influence of its seductive rhythm and fully accept our authentic truths. In it we meld with the earth and connect with the mystical. We are one with what we are. Nothing more, nothing less, nothing expected.

I write my journey to this song. To the revelation of what I am and the constant evolution of my soul, so that you may know that you are not alone. That there is someone out there, in me, a part of this world, breathing the same air and dancing under the same moon and stars as you. They're here. For you.

In the beginning they say there was nothing. I say there was Chaos. Mass. Beauty. Power.

Through this, consciousness was birthed with the desire to expand and grow, to experience and experiment. In your beginning there was brilliance. Light, dark, and desire. Let's start with a story, a mythical character named Angia who represents many of us before the birth of our human form.

The Story of Angia and the Simple Story of the Soul

Angia was a soul in a state of energy. Floating not above, nor below the earthen realm, but in another existence completely.

Her colors, dark blues and dazzling greens, would radiate out around her, touching the darkness of the void and sending tendrils of energy into creation.

Yet, her spirit consciousness, a vast blanket of awareness, longed to grow, to be able to reach farther and burst planets into being, turning aspects of the void into creations of her own making.

She hungered to be a creator. To evolve.

Grasping to her desire to expand, her energy began to tremble. Particles of her being flew together, becoming denser until she held form. Not quite human, but with the outline resembling that species.

A platform opened to her and stairs appeared, she followed them, twisting up, down and around until her consciousness became so confused that it collapsed and re-awoke in a space not far beyond the earth.

Other beings waited there, ideas in hand, hopes for learning. A plan to exist with others in a form which brought more physical restrictions, but with it, an opportunity to test the wisdom they held and develop a further understanding of the clash of energetic chemistry.

Seeing a familiar sigil of greens, she moved toward a tribe of souls she had traveled with before. She sent out a greeting through a warm light.

Moments, hours, or eons may have passed, but in this form, it was nothing. She waited strategically for the time to step down into the human realm.

During this period of patience, she watched, witnessed, and learned the human realm. Partnerships were formed in the ethereal plane and plans were created. Parents chosen, siblings sought out and lovers lined up to provide her new experiences and explosive growth.

A chime tolled within her system and she knew the time had come. Bracing herself for the journey that would seem like a thousand years, but would only be a glimpse in the eyes of time,

she readied herself to become heavier,

weighted by a body, limited by movement.

An earthly entity approached, in shades of brown and red, pointing her attention to a scene appearing before her. A woman in a room, it seemed white. Although others surrounded this female, her heart felt alone. She had no partner sharing in this birth experience with her, but soon she would have Angia to move through life with her.

Breathing in all life as only a spirit can, she sang a note outward, matching the chimes within. The sound reverberating through her entire form until it dissolved her. A vacuum opened to take her swiftly into human form.

A mating occurred, not of two people but of cosmos and earth. Fire rained down on her as a mind took form, intensity became her reality as a squeezing sensation took over her awareness. With the last breath of her spirit, she took one final glimpse of her soul self... allowing it to fade into a distant memory until she returned home or until she chose to awake in her human self.

Angia had chosen to surrender herself to the adventures of the human experience. To walk the zoo of humanity.

She selected a mother that would pass on the necessary genetics required for her to fulfill her path. To attract the lovers, to own certain skills. To provide certain locked-in exploits.

She would have the ability to refuse certain DNA traits that would bring her no joy, and to heal ancestral conditionings that were not hers to bear, but to do this she would need to awaken to her ability to select which she would carry.

Working with the earth, a body was formed as the vehicle.

Her mind formed through her own making to become the interpreter and communication device allowing her to engage others.

Finally, a space in the subconscious was placed between the mind and the soul. A space that, although vulnerable to outside conditioning, would also help her function effortlessly in daily life and absorb information rapidly where her conscious mind could not.

She was birthed. Human. Yet she remained a spirit merely animating a form.

You have your own unique spiritual fingerprint and are similar to Angia, in that you have selected a life, a body, and formed a mind. You're a masterpiece formed from earth and melded with something just outside of our current understanding. You are magick made manifest.

In fact, every aspect of your being is something to be honored, honed, and celebrated.

Walk with me through the jungle of the spiritual to arrive at a hidden temple you've always known existed but didn't know how to find. The roadmap is here, and you hold the key.

Part One – Flirtation of the Cosmos

I heard the whisper on a moonless night
A calling that brushed against my ear teasing my skin
The air seemed to chill as I stopped to listen
Reaching my heart towards the whispers
Goosebumps covered my arms as I felt the room fill
The space around me becoming crowded with the presence of others
Branches scratched against the panes of the windows
and I shivered.
I was not alone. Never alone. Neither are you.
Let me show you.

What You'll Gain

The flirtation of the cosmos will take you on a journey introducing you to your cosmic cheering squad, helping you to wake up and realize you're not alone.

It will help you recognize synchronicities, so that you're tapped into something bigger. Something there supporting you and nudging you forward onto your optimal path.

Learning to use meditation will help you to open up, while quieting your inner dialogue enough to start hearing your eternal self and the cosmos whispering to you. Meditation is foundational to this entire experience.

By the end of this part of your journey you will be happily surrendering to your support system. You'll be capable of learning to receive from the Universe, while feeling confident that you're worthy of that support.

The Seduction of the elements

Did you feel that breeze making its way across your skin? That raindrop kissing your cheek? It's nature's embrace, reaching out to you to remind you of the bliss of simply being.

The earth is constantly revealing her beauty to us and hidden within that radiance there is wisdom. Yet for us to be able to truly see, hear, and understand the messages she is passing forth we must learn to first 1) notice and then 2) listen.

When is the last time you were out for a walk and stopped to touch a tree? (Don't worry about the passersby, part of the journey is becoming comfortable with yourself without caring about others' opinions... and hey, I bet by the next block they'll be doing the same thing.) How often have you actually stopped to smell a rose, a freshly bloomed flower, to run your fingers across the velvety texture of the petals?

We have become so rushed in life. Timetables squeezed with

to dos. Smartphones chiming at us with reminders. The noise of our world has cast a shadow on the mystic beauty and hidden whispers of the natural realm.

And wow, are we ever missing out. You see, there are hidden gems found within our waking world, waiting to pass on insights. Not only is nature hoping we will find our way back to her embrace, but the cosmos is constantly trying to grab our attention.

They are flirting with us. Every synchronicity a wink. Every gut instinct a caress. Hoping to catch our attention.

I find there are days even the grass calls to me. Whispering a need to be touched, appreciated. Those are the times I can be found barefoot wandering through my yard or a park connecting with that which calls to me.

The more you practice opening to the natural magic around you and within you, the longing of the realm to be noticed enhances. The volume turned up. And it begins to seep into your daily life moments, filling them with a renewed sense of peace and belonging. Not necessarily within the human sphere but within this earthly plane.

Every element is alive, has a vein of energy tied into it. The earth, the air, fire, and water. They feed us and fuel us and are willing to offer us guidance or insights if we listen. As I moved through my C Experience, I started to wake up each morning, to greet the world, literally by going out on our deck and saying, "Good morning, World," then I would kneel by a plant that had become a bit of a mini altar for me, and thank each element for their gifts.

Think on it, the earth feeds us and provides us a home, the water carried us out into the world, and we consist of 73% of this beautiful element. The fire is our spirit and passion, plus the sun nourishes us and the air greets us in our first breath on the planet and continues to sustain us daily. Try to give thanks to them, open to them and hear their wisdom.

Your Cosmic Cheering Squad

Have you ever loved someone from afar? Watched them, encouraged them (even silently), and supported them whenever they needed? Have you given yourself to another, and felt that they never truly saw you?

Imagine your teen years with your class crush.

Were you seemingly invisible to someone you loved?

Now, understand. Since your birth, there have been lovers-of-you surrounding you. Unconditional love pouring forth from them into you. They cheered for you, cried with you, handing ethereal Kleenexes your way.

Yet you may not have seen them or ever known they were next to you. But they have always been there loving you.

That is the essence of your cosmic support system. All your life they have waited. During all of your turmoil, your most difficult challenges and your personal victories. They've been waiting for you to realize that they were there, placing steppingstones on your path to take you further. Eagerly anticipating the opportunity to take you into the moonlit moments of the self.

For me, these guides have shown themselves as two predominant figures, my mother and grandmother, both from previous lives. You'll see mention of them throughout my Mystic Moments, most often referred to as my mama or mamas. The connection with them has gone beyond the past physical life, and I've been able to carry and nurture it through to this life.

So, What is Channeling?

Channeling is like being a bridge, literally a channel between unseen realms and this one. When you or I perform the role of a channel, we open up our energetic fields to receive messages from beings (ancestors, helping spirits, guides, other selves) in alternate realms.

During this journey I've included unique glimpses into my mystic journeys and channelings which I've lovingly named

"Mystic Moments".

The messages come through in various formats. They can come through via visuals (clairvoyance), hearing the words in your mind (clairaudience), or simply knowing, similar to gut instinct (claircognizance) and emotions or feelings (clairsentience).

Let's try an exercise together. I'm going to list a few words below, notice what you experience.

Green Pear

Yellow Banana

Apple Pie

Did you see the pear? Could you taste the banana? Did you smell the pie? Did you simply feel its presence?

If you *saw* a shiny green pear, you're more clairvoyant.

If you heard the word "pear" and could even stretch to hear the fruit being munched on, you're more clairaudient.

If you sensed the apple pie, if it brought up emotions or familiar associations, you're more clairsentient.

If you just knew the pear was there, you're more claircognizant.

When I channel, it's as if I'm making a phone call to another realm and am not always certain who will pick up the other end. There are times I can direct it, like a speed dial to a power animal, ancestor, or cosmic guide. But other times, I will open up just to listen and hear if there are any specific insights or messages I should pay attention to.

The majority of my messages come in first as claircognizant, like a hint or a hunch, then they detail themselves out in clairsentient and then clairvoyant formats.

You channel to hear the whisperings of the other realms. To hear guidance and insights that can help you (and/or your loved ones). Although both meditation and channeling can be used to gain answers and clarity, meditation differs as its focus is on quieting the mind and stilling the internal voices so you can find a place of balance within and can receive the messages during a channeling.

If your mental clutter is loud and dominant, imagine that it's like a radio blasting within you, echoing off the chambers of your mind, until it's all you can hear. How can you then receive other frequencies that may be trying to come through to help you? And yes, they are there. They are there for all of us, including you!

Mystic Moments

I dreamt of her again last night, her strong rich voice singing in an ancient language I only recall when I am deep in trance.

I sat outside on the grass watching her weave what looked to my child self like a spider web. Resting a wooden tool on her lap as she sang, her hands expertly braiding the silver and blue strands together from the center out to the ends of the circular object, back to the center, and out again.

Although she smiled at me when she caught me watching her, her golden eyes with tints of green looked like windows into another realm. Her soul seemed to be soaring somewhere amongst the stars.

She was lost in ritual. Bathing in ecstasy of weaving her reality.

The sky was rich with pinpricks of light, the moon new, leaving the land in a sense of beautiful darkness. The space around her seemed to bend, I still don't know if these were tricks of my eyes or if there was truly a soft light embracing her.

My mother has always haunted my mind, memories of her soaking my heart with feelings of joy for her passion and sorrow for all that I lost when she let me go.

And yet this was so long ago. Thousands of years have passed and I still feel her presence as if she has only just left the room.

Your Basic Guide to Meditation

What You'll Gain

One of the major keys you'll need to journey inwards is the gift of meditation. If you've been resistant to meditating in the past, I encourage you to let go of old ideas around what meditation means and uncover your own beautiful way to connect with the true you.

In meditation you're watching your mind and you're interested in the nature of your current state. For example, a mindfulness meditation is often used to focus on one element, such as your breath. This can help you to become less reactive, by watching your own thoughts and perceptions.

This is different from journeying, in which you enter a deep meditative state, but you're focused on the experience and the content. In Shamanic journeying you engage with the storyline. The goal is always to "take your senses with you" when you journey so you can experience the story as it unfolds.

Meditation isn't just a building block for your mystic development, it's a channel. It's the tunnel we pass through to meet our spirit guides, it's the inner ear we employ when listening to our divine selves. It's the gateway to mysticism and in this gateway we can paint the walls of our reality.

In traditional spiritual practices you will meet meditation in its most basic format (or as some of my students have called it "grade 1 spiritual tools"). It's commonly focused on quieting the mind, stilling the body and opening to oneness. Unless you dive into the more mystic realms of magick or new age streams of living, meditation is not utilized to go beyond the "void".

Now it's time to undress this viewpoint of meditation, to take away the structures created to fit a "norm" and rediscover the power of meditation when transformed into a much deeper state termed "trance" or "gnosis". Whereas meditation is about being aware of your mind and not engaging with it, trance is a state you enter in order to connect with something, such as universal energy, a guide, or even what the native referred to as Great Mystery.

Undressing Meditation

As we dive into this practice, I know that many of you are already nodding sagely with a familiarity with meditation, just as some of you are cringing slightly at the idea of "just another person" telling you to sit in lotus (a standard meditation position for yoga lovers) with eyes closed and simply don't think or move. Take a deep breath and relax. I confess, and you will find, I'm not a traditionalist (with meditation being one of the areas). I realize that your soul is so unique that even widely accepted practices of meditation need to be modified to suit your unique spiritual fingerprint.

Having taught thousands of students to meditate, there has been one consistent whispering from my Inner Divine Diva, that for every one person out there who can softly drift into that place of stillness, there are many others struggling, perhaps even engaging in a battle of mind over body.

Let me pass on a secret – it's okay.

Know why? Meditation in its traditional format is not for everyone. It's not perfect for everybody. In fact, it's not the optimal style for many souls. (Was that a gasp?)

Let me explain.

There are hundreds of traditional styles of meditation, all preaching a specific formula for success. They give you a:

- way to sit
- specific focus
- list of "do nots"
- an idea of common experiences.

Now, I think there's one thing we can all agree on, we are all stunningly unique. If I were to compare my unique spiritual fingerprint to yours, they would each have their own radiant design.

Which means that traditional meditation structure is just not for everyone. Perhaps, the reason your meditation practice hasn't been working for you is that your sensational soul is saying, "Listen this just isn't my style." It's time to become conscious of those whisperings and try a new approach.

To truly get the most from your meditation experience, try this –

- **Open Your Inner Ears** – It's time to listen to your Soul Self, she's your inner guru and knows what will bring you the most rewards. Ask her if your current practice is ideal for you. How? Simply take a few breaths, bring the concept of your practice forward and listen inwardly. Does it feel good? Are there aspects that feel right? Or is something just not clicking?
- **Bend the Rules** – Meditation is a spiritual experience, so who put all these human rules on it? No, you don't have to sit in lotus position, lying down is acceptable! Yes, you can dance in meditation (check out the Sufis and ancient tribal traditions), energy is in constant motion so moving your body in sync with its rhythm is a form of meditation. Be willing to adjust elements to make it fit your spiritual makeup.
- **Cut & Paste** – Get crafty with your practice. Select components from other formats which feel good to you and reformulate your own. If you love journeying during your meditation (example visualizing yourself in a healing space) and also find what affirmations work for you, mix them together and create your own. It's fun and irrefutably effective. Plus, it allows you to play with

spirituality which is a beautiful thing.

- **Quiet the Inner Jury** – Smile inwardly during your experience and remember this is not a regimen, it's a lifestyle, a budding relationship between you + your Spirit + the Universe. If you start rating yourself on your meditation practice you defeat the purpose before you even begin.
- **Employ the Mind** – The mind is a tool, thus it needs to feel useful, so give it a job during meditation. I often teach my clients and students to say, "Mind, I want you to sit back, relax and not interfere, but just watch, listen and learn." Allow the mind to be the camerawoman during your experience, taping it, but not assessing it in any way.
- **Dance with Your Spirit** – As you go deeper into your practice remember to not just focus on quieting the mind but listening and savoring an engaging relationship with your soul. We often forget that meditation is just the first step toward a trance, and from trance we can touch the cosmos, converse with our Spirit, dance with the elements and manifest our reality with ease.
- **Open the Dam** – Emotion often acts as the voice of our subconscious. During meditation those walls we've built up between our mind, subconscious, and Spirit come down. Sometimes this feels like a dam bursting open. Let it out. Whether you laugh, cry, or scream, release it. Know that your Guides are always there with a box of spiritual Kleenex, wiping your tears and cheering you forward.

Meditation is not about how great you are at it, or how long you can sit in stillness; it's about what it does for you, mind, body, and Soul. Meditation gives you permission to play with your own formula. Try out different methods, mix them up, and enjoy the experience! Every time you do, you're blossoming a more conscious relationship with your inner Self. You're honoring and listening to that inner knowing first and foremost, not attempting to remold your Spirit to fit a human tradition but taking the wisdom of that Spirit and creating one that is perfect for you.

Client's Story

I had a client in Australia that was struggling with her meditation practice. She was what you might call a "Type A" personality. She liked structure and felt that rigid control was required for success. She was regularly exploring various meditation "disciplines" and processes, reading books, taking seminars, and doing online meditations. Yet, her practice wasn't progressing. We started to explore what was going wrong together. Once we begin to look at our spirituality as a discipline, we've lost the magick of it, we're subconsciously stuffing it into the same category as "having to wash the dishes" or "going to school." She was blocking her free-flowing passion.

The key to shifting her practice into something fulfilling and transformative was based on a few simple adjustments:

1) Literally smiling outwardly and inwardly at the start of her practice.
2) Changing her mindset and language from "regiment" to investing in a budding relationship with herself.
3) Letting go of a rating scale based on how long she sat, or what she felt she achieved (which defeats the purpose of simply savoring peace).
4) Starting fresh with a new approach to letting go of the feelings of failure she had carried around meditation because she was comparing her practice to what she read about in books.

After making these adjustments, she claimed her Soulphoric state with bliss and joy. She found a way to move through life with a sense of liberation and the ability to drop into meditation when she chose.

I once read how Osho said comparison was like placing a Bamboo Tree next to an Oak and asking which was the more worthy or beautiful. The comparison is pointless. Stop subconsciously competing with the others in your yoga class, meditation workshop or even online influencers who *claim* to meditate two or more hours a day. Instead, focus on you because in the end it's not a race, it's about curiosity for your soul.

So, go ahead, reformulate that practice and take notes on what works for you! I would love to hear what specific techniques you respond to.

Mystic Moments

Today I decided to write about channeling but that turned into a spontaneous journey, where I sat outside on the deck to feel my root grounded to the earth. I asked my Mamas about channeling. They responded that it's a bridge and then I had an interesting epiphany and decided to ask them who they would use to channel if I channeled them. Threads of light came down towards me and lights gathered as they came closer, blending into one beam of light, one thick cord. When it touched my head, it melted down around me, embracing my body while entering into me. I then felt it go out my roots and spread into the earth like tree roots that turned me into a tree. I became my legacy of light tree.

When I came back to the present moment, I looked around and everything seemed brighter. Life sparkled.

Who did they channel is an interesting question. And how did they channel? It's time for this knowledge to come forward.

Was it a pantheon, and who were they? Or the Universal Mother, who I believe I met in a dream healing as a veiled being with foamy light green skin.

Part One Practices – Flirtation of the Cosmos

Practice 1 – Connecting to the Elements

It's time to connect with the energy of the elements. Feel the earth below you supporting you, the water running through you, the fire igniting your passion and the air nurturing you!

1. Get ready to go outside, shoes on, keys by the door (put your phone down).
2. Stand or sit comfortably, spine straight and take a few deep breaths.
3. Feel your body and mind waking up to your attention.
4. You may even incorporate in here the smiling inwardly exercise from the Body component.
5. Now look down at your feet and notice them connected to the ground (whether it's carpet, or wood or tiles), and open consciously to the energy of the earth flowing up through you.
6. Now imagine that energy moving up your spine, straight to the top of your head and expanding outwards about ½ foot around your body.
7. Breathe in 3 more times.
8. Now head outside, and notice the air, the feel of it. Notice it filling your lungs and nourishing you.
9. Is the sun out? If so, thank it for its warmth, and if not, still greet it even if it is hidden behind clouds.
10. Do you have a tree nearby or even a plant or bush? Notice if one calls to you; you'll feel as if it is reaching out and saying, "Notice me." Once you have one you can feel would like your attention, move towards it.
11. At this point, I like to hug the trees (yes, I actually hug them) and lean against them. Thank the tree for being a tree, and let it know you feel it is doing a good job.
12. Now stop and listen.

13. Listen to the tree.
14. Listen to what's happening within you.
15. Listen and notice.

Repeat the above but rotate through the elements. For example, I live close to a lake; when connecting with water, I will go down and dip my toes into the lake. If you don't have a body of water in close proximity, then wait for the rain. When it rains go outside and be in it. Feel it. Listen to what it stirs within you.

For the wind, I've discovered sitting outside when the wind is loud and howling allows me to connect with the essence of it; this opens me to have the wind blow through me to help me clear the (mental, emotional, physical) clutter.

But each time, no matter which element I connect with, I always do two things:

1. Thank it for its gift of life it brings.
2. Listen to it, tuning in to hear if it has anything to whisper back to me or show me.

Practice 2 – Discovering Divine Winks (Synchronicity)

Take a moment and list out three times you've experienced synchronicity (positive or negative). When you start to appreciate what shows up, more and more will come.

You can pull more positive synchronicity into your life:

1. Recognize when you have an experience that could be synchronistic.
2. Recognize the positive impact it has had on your life.
3. Thank the universe or element or guides (whomever you work with) for this gift.
4. Make space within your energy field to receive more.

Often the most forgotten is number 4. The ability to make space in your life and allow the universe to do the work. If you're like most people (including myself) you probably feel like you need to be going, going, going – forgetting that rest is also part of the formula. It's important that we allow the Universe to do its part, and we know and embrace that it will all work out. Letting go of how it will all unfold is necessary too since, if we hold on too tight to how it SHOULD look, we are not giving free rein to the Universe to weave its magic.

Making space can be done by doing yoga (imagine each stretching sensation is creating space within you), deep breathing (with every exhale, release), and being in stillness (or meditation), feeling yourself opening, softening to receiving.

The Cosmos is flirting with you (perhaps even right now), so start flirting back by seeing the synchronistic events happening in your life and blowing them a kiss to say thanks. And when the unpleasant ones come up, take a deep breath, and reevaluate your next steps (and still send a kiss to the universe for putting you back on track).

Practice 3 – Breathing Tips for Meditations

Breathing tips – these tips will help you to learn a few breaths we'll use going forward as well as different styles of breathing which can help you relax and calm your mind (to better experience the Flirtation of the Cosmos).

Each breath should be done via your nostrils, until you get the relaxed breath which can be released out through your mouth.

Breath Descriptions

Step Breath: This is when we inhale up through our body, as each breath is a step going up a vertebra. We continue to inhale until we need to release it or until we reach the top of our crown.

Bellow Breath: This is where we add our breath to one part of our body as if we are fanning the flame with it. These are done with short quick exhales; you will feel your abdomen pulling in sharply as you perform this breath.

Relaxed Breath: This is a relaxed and releasing exhale. Shake it all out, feel good.

Part Two – Embodying the Soul

The spirit looked down upon the earth and whispered,

"If I could only discover the taste of honey. To have a tongue to lick it off my loved one.

To know the experience of goosebumps across my skin.

To realize the sensations of death and birth, adrenaline and calm.

To know the extremes without knowing that this is what I know.

To realize the gift I have when I am not asleep but awake."

Embodying the Soul

To be of the soul we must also be of the body. Every cell within our being is one with our soul self. Every breath we take, every touch we share, every food we taste is part of the soul's experience. Nothing is separate. To believe that segregation exists between body and soul, is to lie to yourself about the value of this form you inhabit.

Without the body we cease to experience this world.
Our Souls free float around the earth like wisps of air or are racing upwards into the cosmic energy.

When treated with love, your body is a key to a fulfilled life, it's one of the three aspects that unlock the gift of a Soulphoria, allowing your spirit self to experience the sensuality of living.

We Breathe. We Dance. We Feast. We Make Love.

Our Soul revels and grows through experiences. They are a gift to our spirit evolution and are an integral part of why we chose to be a physical incarnation versus a spirit floating around the atmosphere.

Your body wants to feel loved. Think of a child who comes from a good home with decent parents, the child is well fed, but no one takes the time to play with her, no one tells her they love her or engages with her to challenge her growth. So, the child as she ages becomes depressed, and it shows.

This child is like your body; it wants to play and you're responsible for providing the spectrum of opportunities and activities through which it can express itself. It's up to you to ensure the body is well fed, but more than that, that it's loved, and appreciated and given the opportunity to love life with you.

The results go beyond feeling good. You actually start to tune in and hear your body asking you for specific food or nutrients it needs, while also making you aware of when you shouldn't be consuming something through gut instincts. Your body starts to open and share things with you, just as a child would. Imagine a child being recognized for the first time, and smiling back at you, that's what your body will do.

Mystic Moments

Today as I flowed through my yoga practice, I felt the old nagging of my mind, "You should be working, you should be writing, you should be doing something financially productive."

However, this time, I found myself asking my body if this is what it would like, and the answer was clearly, "No." My body showed me how unhappy it would feel sitting back at the computer. In that moment I realized that if I did remove myself to go and write, disrupting my physical form's flow, I would most likely get so fidgety that I wouldn't be able to focus and would have nothing to say.

I saw each decision like a funneling column of light and as I decided to stay on my mat, I saw my body, mind and soul self slide into one, making a pure channel for life and all its beautiful parts. This is the way I check in with my decisions. This was an awakening for me, as finishing my flow gave my body what it wanted. I can feel it smiling at me as I sit and write about this.

Your Body Blueprint

What You'll Gain

Time to begin healing your relationship with your body and claim the beautiful "you" you've chosen to be in this life. You are your own masterpiece.

Just as Angia carefully selected her physical form, you chose your own corporeal makeup. Your spirit's incredible wisdom intuited what would be needed to embark and fulfill your current expedition.

Before you were born you selected the perfect location for you to enter (the country you're born in), you chose the optimal channels for your birth (your parents and ancestry, providing you specific cells, traits, skills), you glimpsed the path your family would take (where you would move and end up as an adult) and finally worked with the dense energy of this reality (earth energy) to mold and sculpt a body that would be ideal for the specific adventures you would have in this life.

Your Spirit was the artist and you its masterpiece.

I know some of us wish our forms would have been constructed as more of a high performance or luxury vehicle. From this moment forward, you know different. This is the day you begin to accept your body's perfection, not in comparison to the world around you, but as the optimal host and vehicle for you.

The reflection you spot in the mirror may not always be your mind's ideal appearance – but your soul never wishes you had brown eyes, a bigger smile or straighter hair. Your body is a unique work of art, sculpted from the earth's solidness by the hands of your Spirit. And now, your Spirit wishes to be allowed to taste this world through the body it formed. Let's enter the garden of your soul.

Tending Your Inner Garden

What You'll Gain

Uncover the fertile soul within you and tend to your inner garden to make it a luscious sanctuary where your Soulphoria can grow.

The body is the fertile soil in which we plant our Soulphoria seeds. Through nurturing our physical form, we bloom into unique and radiant blossoms, our branches reaching out to share our vivacity with the world around us, while receiving love like sunlight.

When the soil is not filled with healthy nutrients (loving your body, and appreciating the gifts it brings, and allowing yourself to truly live through it), it grows weeds. These are destructive thoughts which choke our budding flora or other people's negativity which stifle our buds from blooming.

Weeding the soil takes a commitment to yourself and the permission to finally celebrate being in a physical form. It also requires letting go of limiting beliefs that have caused us to see our body as a showcase for sin, temptation, or destruction.

Many popular religious views and philosophies will ask you to shut down the desires of the flesh. What Soulphoria requires is quite different – passion for the physical and the joy of savoring this world through tangible experiences.

The body is of the earth, and thus it's animalistic in nature. Yet, it's only out of control when it's not led by the soul self.

Think of a loving pet. You care for it, adore it, nurture it and you also teach it how to behave. You channel its natural instincts in the direction that's appropriate. However, when it's abandoned or ignored that pet can get out of control, reverting back to its own survival instinct.

On the other side, if we only discipline that pet, train it, work it, without love, it will become defensive, non-receptive and guarded. You'll never have a positive relationship, nor will you experience any of the joy that comes with it.

The real goal is to bond your soul with your body, learn to hear the body's voice, spend time appreciating your physical form, so you can finally embody the soul in daily life, experiencing what a sensual journey life can be.

To achieve this, begin the process of absorbing your awareness into your entire physique. Don't get trapped in your head. Feel through your body more intensely, letting sensation trickle down your spine, melt through your limbs and tingle in your fingers and toes. Just like orgasm, to achieve Soulphoria the body must be in a receptive state, soft, fluid, and ready.

The body can't exactly feel the intricacies of every emotion, it works mostly through pain and pleasure. The survival instinct leads to fear, which snaps you out of your body and into your mind.

Learn to Listen and Connect to Your Beautiful Body

The body is a symphony, filled with a wonderful series of rhythms, melodies, and harmonies – the sound of our hearts beating, the rush of blood through our veins, the electrical currents moving through our nervous systems.

The deeper we go hearing our body's song, the more we are able to intuit our unique needs for a healthy life and awaken the presence of the soul self in every cell of our physical makeup, allowing for our spirit to tangibly touch the world. We can nurture fertile soil for our life experiences from which we can then learn how to work with its unique nature and discover our spirit self within its depths.

Let's begin with a meditation on hearing the body. This meditation came to me as a memory from another lifetime, a practice which I understand was part of the initial stages of an ancient initiation. Regardless of its roots, it's a powerful tool.

I've included my channeled meditation below and will

provide you with your own step by step guide following.

Your Turn. Let's Connect You Back into Your Body.

Weeding the Garden

Life has a way of providing us with a few bumps and bruises along the way that we can use to learn. Whether emotional or physical, these can turn into scars that affect how we view ourselves and the world around us unless we work to heal ourselves at the soul level.

Your body can go into a crisis mode when you allow the past to continue to impact on you, giving your power over to it, or focus on fears of the future. Those moments when you're back in the trauma of the past or thrust into the unknowns (and fears) of the future, your body can freeze and feel whomped by the stress energies. In Part 3 we'll talk about how to heal mental blocks in depth, but this will give you a way to get started.

Comparison has been one of my personal weeds. I've heard this called "comparanoia", when you think *everybody* is better off than you. It's one of the most insidious weeds out there, and it can wreak havoc on your confidence and body image. It can lead to conscious and subconscious abuse of your physicality and even manifest itself as illness and disease.

Working through weeding your soil takes time. To believe it should happen in an instant is a form of self-sabotage. As you move through the exercises found in this book, remember to go slow and have patience, otherwise, you will experience a sense of failure. This is why it's so important to commit to a practice of self-love.

As you get more comfortable and go deeper into the process, there may be a flash of sudden understanding or an epiphany, but even that takes time to be grounded and "massaged" into daily life.

Have you ever experienced those "aha" moments, when you finally feel healed, or you've gained understanding, or see the world through new eyes? Often, after a few days that "aha" seems to have faded. It takes time to integrate this new way of being into your life. A spiritual experience or sudden awakening can change you forever, but it's up to you to make it a part of the rest of your moments thereafter.

Weeding is an ongoing process. Be gentle with yourself yet firm, meaning no excuses, and loads of self-acceptance.

My personal launch forward towards healing my relationship with my body came one day in the shower. Out of the blue I heard that old voice of comparison which had been lurking in the back of my mind. It started to berate me, "You're just not as liberated as so and so. You're not nearly as sexy as she is. You're nothing compared to the others. You're a mistake for anyone to be with except for a one-night stand. They dream of all these other women and you will never compare."

Tears began to flow down my cheeks. I pressed my hand against the glass of the shower and rested my head there. I cried, while in my mind I turned to face the voice. It was in a fog. I couldn't see who was speaking, nor could I tell if it was a man or a woman. It just was someone out there, yet in my head.

As I went to say, "Enough!" I found myself standing in the middle of a massive circle of females within my mind's eye.

As I turned in the circle, I saw a hologram of myself running to my left to become more like the female over there, then that projection of "I" ran back across the circle to my right to look more like the woman standing there. She ran and ran trying to absorb the understanding of how to be good enough, how to be more like them so I would be *something*. Then I collapsed.

I could not win.

I could not be all of them.

In that moment I looked and saw how different each one was, that they also weren't like one another. They weren't perfect. They may have had beauty or intrigue in their own unique ways, but not one of them had it all. Yet here I was torturing myself into believing something was wrong with me. The fact was that other people's reactions to me had been because of their own inner upheaval and fears.

The women turned and faded out. I saw myself in the center and finally got a glimmer of the true me. There was something special there, something radiant. I didn't know what, but I could sense it. It was like the light was playing tricks with my eyes and I could see a sparkle dancing around me, coaxing me to look closer at myself.

There was beauty in me, somewhere deep inside and if I didn't ever discover it and share it, no one would ever be able to love me for who I was. They would be loving the copied energy I wore to make myself "worthwhile".

No one could love me if I never allowed them to see me.

I finally wanted my body to be appreciated as it was. My body deserved it and so did my soul.

You deserve it too.

However, for you and your body to be loved it has to start with self-respect. Loving yourself isn't just an internal affair, it's also a physical one.

Forgiveness of the self often starts with tears.

Loving Your Body

What You'll Gain

It's time to build out a new relationship with your body. Discover the beauty that is you through your own experience of tactile self-love.

Caring for the Body

Aaah, the bliss of a body that's thriving. The body in its raw form is one of earth's treasures. It's an animal, and like an animal it has basic needs which must be honored in order for it to provide us with a beautiful ride through this life.

Don't worry, I'm not about to lecture on the dos and don'ts. I believe when you're tuned in, you can discover what is best for your body and learn to listen to its purring or growling. You learn to recognize what is nurturing for your physical matrix.

Not everyone is meant to be a vegetarian (I'm not), nor can everybody tolerate things like dairy (my system rejects it like it was diesel, a toxic substance). The key is to tune inwards and build on what you learn by listening to your body.

There are three main ingredients to creating a beautiful relationship with your body, they're the pillars for Soulphoria:

1) Sleep
2) Movement
3) Nourishment

Sleep

The lack of proper sleep can stall any progress you make toward a thriving physical form and the ability to achieve Soulphoria. In fact, without proper rest, the whole world begins to look skewed. A study by Harvard Health has shown that not enough sleep can cause depression, especially in women, due to an imbalance in hormones. On average we need between 6-8 hours of rest. However, if you're handling stress and multitasking, you'll need even more sleep. Take time to reflect on your personal sleep patterns.

If you're not getting enough shut eye, this needs to be the first phase of your body loving program.

1) Create a nighttime ritual before bed. I call it sleep foreplay; it's a time when you know a gratifying night of healing, rejuvenation and mini detoxing is just an hour away.

    a. Make a list of the To Dos that are weighing on you and put them away, far from your sleeping space. Note that you will deal with them on the morrow and therefore don't need to think about them for the night.

    b. Ensure that all electronics are shut off at least 30 minutes before you turn in.

    c. Take time to enjoy a relaxing activity – read a light book, have a bath, do some gentle stretching, yoga, or qi gong.

    d. Play soothing music to help you unwind.

    e. Give your body a loving massage.

    f. Take a few moments just as you're unwinding and closing your eyes to list three things you are grateful for.

2) As you get into bed, take a few deep breaths and release any remaining tension or stress.

    a. Don't worry about doing serious or focused meditation before bed when you're aiming for a simply restful night. This can cause activity in your dreams that may rob you of that wakefulness in the morning.

    b. Find a soothing color that creates a sensation of

peace within you. Feel yourself falling backwards onto it, allowing your body to melt into its embrace. Notice how you sink deeper into the mattress and how your head is cradled by the pillow.

c. Give yourself permission to let go and tell your body that this is a time for healing and sleep.

Movement

Dancing, qi gong, yoga, hiking whatever your personal preference, find it and do it! Movement is a necessary part of not only creating a healthy form, but also exploring the world around you.

During my big C Experience and still to this day, I've learned that movement is not just for making us feel better about the external self we're presenting to the world, but it's also a critical part of keeping yourself sane and reducing stress. Movement has become my key to finding peace when my thoughts are too loud, or even when everything is so quiet within, I'm lost over what to do with myself. Movement and my body have become two of my best friends. I move when I'm stressed, when I'm sad, when I'm frustrated, confused... I move when I'm happy and joyful, I move to celebrate my life and body, and I move to celebrate the planet.

If you're stuck for how to bring renewed energy into your life, physical movement is the groundwork on which you can build.

Nourishment

As a hedonist I love great food. I find that dairy-free hazelnut gelato hums an enchanting harmony and deep dark chocolate chants a rhythm my taste buds instinctively move to. However, I am also aware that certain food groups may provide an instant of gratification yet leave my body wishing I would've looked the other way for hours later (like the dairy in a cheesecake).

Food intolerances, allergies or aversions are important to become aware of. Are you uncertain about what doesn't work with your physical makeup? Having your body tested is a worthy investment.

If you're unable to do this, there are simple ways to find out which foods are not serving your health. The most common culprits are dairy, gluten, red meat and of course sugar. Test your body's tolerance by taking 14 days off of each food group (individually – not all at once). Then take notes.

1) How does your body feel at the end of the 14 days?
2) How has your weight changed?
3) Do you notice any inflammation changes?
4) Has your digestion and elimination improved?
5) Do you have more energy?
6) Are you sleeping better?
7) Has your complexion changed?

For over four years I believed that bread was the main challenge for my digestion, until one spring I decided to explore what would happen if I gave up dairy. By the end of the first week, I had friends and family commenting on the change in my complexion and even eye clarity. I soon realized dairy not only affected how I looked, it was also draining me of energy and vitality.

The more you eat in sync with your own specific requirements the better you will feel, look, and live.

As you adopt a healthy self-care plan, you'll be naturally drawn to those things that best serve your body. Your instinctual lifestyle choices will shift to food, activities and physical exchanges that nourish you. In fact, the idea of forcing yourself to give up anything is not important for this experience. Those things that don't feed your soul through the body will eventually drop away.

Partnering with the Earth

What You'll Gain

Here you'll rebuild that delicious, deep connection with the earth, further heal your relationship with your body and become empowered.

The simplest physical experiences, such as a hug, to the most exhilarating exploits are brought to us sponsored by the earth. Through her partnership we taste life and evolve our soul.

When we fear the body, we block its passions and neglect its needs. We refuse its energy which is the source of all life. When we're not nurtured by the earth, we lose our own creativity.

The body is the gateway to the earth energy. It's essential to move through life, strengthening the connection to Gaia. As the manifest form of energy, the things we wish to unfold tangibly are part of a web. Moving through our body we learn to work within the earth's natural flow, as well as weave our own desires into being.

There are beings that move through our realm unanchored to the earth. You're not one of them.

For me, the sound of drums represents the earth. Tribal beats that call me to move in a way that's ancient. They pull up memories that are stronger than societal conditionings and instead call for you to move in the most primal way.

Hips don't just sway, they gyrate. Your soul makes love to the energies of this earth and its many elements.

You are fire.

You are water.

You are earth.

You are air.

You are, and because you exist the earth asks you to dance for it.

Slowly stripping away the definitions of your human

experience, the earth undresses your mind, seducing you to let go. In this there is freedom. You're finally a soul within an earth-gifted form: your body.

Through partnering with the earth, you will realize the beauty of the form you inhabit, the desire to love it and experience all it has to offer. Why? Because you're finally back to looking at it through the eyes of the spirit and not the flittering negativity of the human mind.

What bliss.

Client's Story

In a retreat I was hosting, we were working with energy packages (challenges, problems, issues wrapped up in an envisioned energy packet). Each participant was invited to call upon their child, teen, and woman side to help them identify which aspect could help them heal.

As D held out her energy package (the specific bundle of emotions she was working through), her child side appeared as a little girl, looking so full of sadness. D moved towards her child self and picked her up, holding her. She asked, "What is it?" The little girl cried saying that she felt her daddy had left because of her.

D's father left when she was three years old and shortly afterwards had a baby girl with his new girlfriend. D hadn't realized that her child side had been blaming both herself and her mother for her father leaving.

Her teenage side then popped in and had more anger towards her mother.

For years she has carried this blame. Divorced three times she finally realized the devastation this unconscious self-blame has brought to her life.

Sexual Expression

What You'll Gain

Release any sexual shame and begin to truly enjoy your sexuality. Discover the spirituality in your sexual self.

During my personal journey to Soulphoria and ecstatic self-love, I've met myself in various formats along the way. Traversing the plains of the physical body, I began to uncover my shadowed desires, fetishes, kinks and naughty thoughts (that are naughty no more... it's all how you look at it). I've taken a graceful swan dive into the darkest recesses of my mind where I had hidden what I thought were the "unacceptable" pieces of my sexual nature.

I discovered that these little pieces which I'd put in the shadows and labeled as "no-nos" were delectably divine. By bringing them into the light and looking closer I learned so much more about who I am, where my "negative" conditioning came from and I finally freed myself to embrace my entire being. Liberation of my sexual expression brought me back into the arms of my inner Lover. The Vixen.

Are you free in your sexual self? ... Do you know your deepest desires?

Have you ever experimented with the heart-rousing feeling of knowing yourself and soul in the most intimate of ways? You release your essence through the gift of orgasm, sending energy of bliss into the world for love. This is the soul-filled experience of truly, deeply, and fully making love to the self. The true experience of physical and spiritual self-love.

If you're one of those ladies who have not yet experienced an orgasm, this next section (and the exercises to go along with it!) may make you sigh with delight.

Yes, I'm talking about self-pleasuring (aka masturbation). For those of you who are blushing, relax with me. Take a deep breath and realize that this is a powerful channel to self-knowing. To experience your physical body through touch, is a way of learning how this amazing vehicle loves to be honored, plus it brings a gift of pleasure to your soul self. Allow yourself to drop the suppressive ideas about self-pleasure, and instead commit to enjoying yourself!

It's a cleansing of excess energy and a revitalization of your creativity and passion. The most passionate parts of our creative being reside within our sexuality. They're knotted together like lovers. (There is a reason so many of the world's gifted creatives have had notoriously enormous libidos!)

There are so many different styles of sexual repression. I've even heard an ugly rumor floating around the spiritual community that you only have so much sexual energy and creative resources. (This is widely held as a truth within the tantric domains.) This has convinced many to give up seeking sexual fulfillment and reserve those resources for "higher" creativity. Yet, those same individuals believe in the unlimited energy flow of nature and the cosmos, which leads us to the flaw in the theory. The unlimited energy of creative cosmic power is what feeds your passion, thus that boundless source is yours to draw upon. You only need to tap into it.

Your creative and sexual source is not a bank, only holding so many "energy bucks," but instead a river attached to an ocean, always bringing in more. The more we draw from that river, the more fresh energy flows into us. It's a beautiful cycle of rebirth in constant action.

Mystic Moments

During this mystic moment you will come across language most of you will not recognize. Definitions provided at the end of the section.

I look at her eyes watching me, like a cat. They crinkle softly at the corners when she smiles and says, "Close your eyes and choisiana... focus inwards."

I sigh with a mixture of desire to explore my own body and the slight resistance that for some reason comes natural to me. Leaning back against the tree I hear her clear her throat and find myself straightening back up again.

"When you've grasped the exercise, you can use the Hermiosa to sit against. Until then the upright will make you remain here." Hermiosa was our name for the mammoth tree that acted as a canopy of shade from the hot sun.

Sighing again I sat upright, knowing my exhale was simply for show. I was 15 in this vision, attempting to exert myself and make my voice heard.

Closing my eyes again I looked inwards. Seeing the vast cavern of "I" that was like a vacuum for my Soul self. Stepping away from the gateway I knew would take me outwards to the cosmic, I focused on simply breathing.

"Choichi, yes, choisah," inhale and release. I felt soft fabric pressed against my eyelids and allowed any light to be blocked out, bringing my awareness deeper within my body. "Choichi... choisah." My body relaxed outwardly yet an arrow of energy became a solid pillar filling

my core from my crown to my root.

Sensing the energy shift, my mother took my hand and told me to calm. Keep breathing, remain here and placed my palms onto thighs.

"Hear the rhythm of your breath," she said. "Follow it as far as you can to the base of your form. Raise one finger when you have found the end of the breath."

I exhaled deeply and sank within myself, down into my body, until I found the pool of energy that rested at my root. Kriali for women, Krial for men.

I raised a finger and felt my mother begin to fill my ears with a mossy substance. Comfort overtook me. Before she finished blocking out the sounds around me, she said, "Now listen. Hear your body, don't leave it, don't lose it, be in it and know it. Mate your mind to body to Soul."

Choisiana – To focus inwards

Hermiosa – A name for a species of tree with large roots and trunk

Choichi – To inhale

Choisah – To exhale

Kriali – A woman's power energy center (near the root chakra)

Krial – A man's power energy center (near the root chakra)

Part Two Practices – Embodying the Soul

Practice 4 – Befriend Your Body

Reconnecting with your physical body starts with claiming your body as yours. Taking it back.

This is my body.
This is my breath.
This is my mind.
These are my thoughts.
This my spine.

You're awake in this moment in your body, yet you aren't awake in every cell. Most of you is asleep, just as most of your brain is at rest. Your energy body is in a state of partial awareness. When you awaken your whole body, you open up to psychic gifts, delectable sexuality, heightened sensuality and a full understanding of the pain and pleasure of this life experience. You're awake at the point of readiness for Soulphoria, you're alive in the most profound way. You chose life and because of that you become the Creator of it, invested in it without losing yourself through it.

Practice 5 – Grounding Cosmic Energies

Boundless within the Boundaries: Rooting Down the Cosmic to Embrace the Earth

This exercise takes almost a counterintuitive approach to grounding. It's not about going into the earth, as you will only allow your roots to meld in two inches maximum. Instead, it's about bringing your cosmic essence down and embracing the earth with your energy.

You will need:

- a quiet space, somewhere you can relax, exist and just be.
- somewhere comfortable to sit or stand. It's up to you, there is no correct position.

Steps:

1. Starting at the crown of your head (the crown chakra), feel your breath extending upwards and connecting with the cosmic essences. Allow it to merge into your system as you open up the top of your head and make space to bring the energy down into your system.
2. Breathe in a short shallow breath, as you do, connect and feel the cosmic energy entering into your body.
3. Breathe in another short breath (I call this step breaths) and bring the energy down to fill your head. Then continue on with these breaths until you fill your entire body. You'll feel it radiating.
4. Once you get to the soles of your feet, be sure and do a strong exhale out.
5. Bring the exhale down to wrap itself like roots around the earth, not into the earth.

6. Feel your energy embracing the earth's existence and energy forms.
7. Then if you wish, allow your energy to enter into the earth (as roots) an inch or two.
8. Relax here, feel the flow of cosmic (the boundless), to earth (the boundaries).

Practice 6 – Self Sexual Exploration

Can you play with your fantasies, at least in a fantasy land of your making?

If not, try this... no judgement allowed! No one is watching so let go and float in the sexual ocean of your dreams.

1) Give yourself permission to be a fiery, frisky feline for a few moments.

2) Let go of any thoughts of "good or bad," "right or wrong" that your family, friends, past relationships, religions, society may have placed on you, or rather you decided to identify as.

3) Take three breaths and relax with your hands resting on your body, connect with it, honor it. Love it.

4) Ask your inner self and body, what excites you? Don't edit, don't judge. Just listen. Your Spirit may be speaking.

5) Write it down. (Yes, you can hide it somewhere that no one will read it or erase it after.) The key is to see what comes out.

6) Keep practicing this a few times a week. Let yourself be free in the playground of sexual fantasy and kinky bliss.

Doing this fun (and oh so delectable) practice a few times per week will create a tangible change in the relationship with yourself, your body, and your lover(s). As you become more confident and aware of your sexually authentic divine self, your inner life and outer experiences will undeniably open up in all areas.

Practice 7 – Smiling Inwardly Exercise

I've started to do this simple exercise every morning and evening, it's a part of the Chinese healing meditation found in Qi Gong. Basically, sandwiching my day in a beautiful space of self-love. Try it for the next week and note down your experiences with each of the body parts. (I've dropped in a few examples where I show how my relationship with my body and organs changed by going through this process.)

The most challenging part of this is the smiling.

The Process:

1) Get comfortable – you can do this standing or sitting (I used to do this on my treadmill).
2) If it's safe and you're not maneuvering your bike down a busy street, close your eyes.
3) Bring a positive feeling or thought to mind. Now smile at yourself. This may be by you simply lifting the corners of your mouth and tuning your mind inwards or it could be you literally feeling as if you're smiling at something or someone you love, but inwardly.
4) Take two deep breaths.
5) Starting with your brain, feel yourself focusing inwards and smiling at it. Imagine your brain within your skull and open yourself to feel love and appreciation toward it, to feel appreciation for it.
6) Breathe with this for a few moments.
7) Now, bring your attention to your heart and once again, feel it and smile at it. Feel it brighten up and lighten as you put your loving inner gaze on it.
8) Now move your attention down to your kidneys.
9) To your abdomen, and digestive system.

10) To your liver, gallbladder, spleen.
11) To your lungs.
12) To your Immune System.
13) To your Lymphatic System.
14) To your Central Nervous System.
15) To every cell within your body. Smile and be open to noticing.

Jot down your experiences and notice how they evolve and change.

Brain:
The first time I smiled at my brain, it was angry with me. I felt that I couldn't connect with it. Now my brain smiles back, in the form of a light pink glow emanating from it.

Heart:
My heart was really open on my first smiling round. Now my heart feels stronger and can stimulate my other organs to get involved.

Kidneys:
I often hear my kidneys giggling as I do my sound healing. They feel like they are happily keeping my body fluid.

Liver:
My liver at first felt like an old man, grumpy and tired, however, when I turn my attention towards it now, it appears softer, more youthful, and happy.

Immune System:
My immune system has gone from feeling like women aimlessly moving around within me, to now ships of warrior women, patiently watching to defend and protect their domain. My body.

Lymphatic System:
In the beginning my lymphatic wasn't that responsive, but as time went by and with daily practice it was like a little girl and woke up and now she giggles. I often like to feel as if I'm tickling my lymphatic system.

Central Nervous System:
At first, my CNS felt like a stern male who wasn't interested in smiling, but he's loosened up now.

Entire body – Every Cell:
You can try this before you get out of bed in the morning, just as you're waking up. Always keep going, even if you get sidetracked. Keep making this loving cycle all the way through your body. If you need inspiration, think of someone you love or look at something that makes you smile, then turn that energy inwards. Some organs will respond differently, be open to getting to know your body in this more intimate way. Don't give up. Try it for at least a week. You'll see.

Practice 8 – Weeding the Inner Garden

The weeds which grow within can strangle your potential, causing the inner sun of your spirit to be blocked out from nurturing your soil and allowing the fruits of your spirit to blossom. It's time to start removing the weeds to ensure your inner garden is healthy.

Bring your awareness to your physical form and allow yourself to feel alive in it.

Now look yourself over – what is stopping you from identifying with your body and loving it? Allow yourself to go deeply into the layers of mind, body, and soul. Feel your spirit animating a body, which means it's part of your current makeup. It has an important role in this soul adventure.

Write down the top three things that block self-love and body-love:

1.

2.

3.

Now sit back, take a deep inhale, and let it out.

Weeding Phase 2:

Select one of the culprits from above that seem to cause the most negative ripples in your life. The one that blocks your self-expression, stops you from sharing yourself with others, causes self-abuse and/or stops you from experiencing life.

When you have selected the one you believe is the biggest culprit write down the ways it's impacting your life. Make a list of at least five situations, scenarios, relationships or dreams it's blocking.

1.

2.

3.

4.

5.

Allow yourself to feel a sense of "enoughness". This is important! You must feel that you've had enough of this negative imprint in your life. It's time to iron it out.

Say to yourself (in your own words), "I've had enough of this taking _____ from me or stopping me from _____ . I deserve to experience this life through my body, and enough is enough!" Allow yourself to say it again, this time with more emotion – ignite the statement, allow fire from your soul to come flooding forward into the words, "enough is enough!"

Now, give yourself permission to let it go.

If you see the same block reappearing, notice it, face it, say no to it and then walk away from it. To hide from it will allow it to remain, but to argue with it will allow it to grow. You must acknowledge it to strip it of its power.

As you begin this process you will discover shifts within your system. Pay attention to sudden insights, dreams, or inspirations. If you feel drawn to try something new, do it! This is the time to step out and challenge yourself with new activities that you would never have done before. Showing the courage to experience life through the body shrinks the blocks within you as they no longer have the same fear to feed from. In other words, the grip those weeds had on you begin to release until they're no longer there at all.

Practice 9 – Unleash Voice & Free Your Body

This is a perfect (and very fun!) practice for those who feel like their authentic voice is stifled or blocked. It's time to make some noise!

Go find a quiet space, close the door (warn your flat mates, lover or family) and scream, laugh, sing, express yourself! Use your voice and listen to the sounds your body makes when you let loose. Let's hear you growl and purr.

Practice 10 – Find Your Power Within

Inside each one of us is a place of power. This is your center, where you can turn to for solace or when you need a burst of focus or confidence.

1) Find a place where you can have a few moments to yourself. We're going to go on a bit of a journey inward.
2) Relax into a comfortable position. You can lie down, sit up or even stand. (I often like to do this outdoors to use the power of nature.)
3) Start by focusing on your breath. On your inhale, feel your breath being pulled in. Now notice your exhale. Do this for about five breaths.
4) Feel your third eye turn inward, toward yourself. You may also wish to close your eyes at this stage.
5) Place your hands on your belly.
6) Feel the rise and fall of your stomach as you breathe.
7) Allow your shoulders to relax down your back.
8) Bring your attention to your physical form until you feel your body. Picture yourself diving deep into the depths of your being.
9) Relax and breathe.
10) Now ask yourself which part of you holds your power and energy center.
11) Notice which part of your being stands out or feels like it holds additional energy.
12) Allow your consciousness to move to that area and feel like you're snuggling up within it.
13) Breathe.
14) Enjoy the sensation of being connected to your core.
15) Lock it in. Remember this feeling so you can return to it again.

My power center is in my hips, the area of the sacral chakra. Your power center may be in a different part of your body. Go with it, don't judge it. (No judgement allowed during this entire process!) Whatever reveals itself to you, trust it. Distrust can create thick curtains that hide our own truths. We want to remove that curtain to be able to connect with our soul self.

A few tools I will often incorporate include:

- My shamanic drum. Monotonous drumming has been proven to increase the power of the alpha and theta frequencies of the listener. This allows you to slip into and out of trance more easily.
- Lighting a candle or incense can help you shift your space more easily. This is often used in journeying to set the stage before you dive in.

Bonus: For those who prefer a guided version, be sure to visit the Soulphoria site here and download your copy. Then sit back, relax, and let www.soulphoria.ca soothe you into your center. (As always feel free to share with those you think could benefit from it.)

Practice 11 – Loving Your Body

Your body is a gift from the earth, and one we want to care for (like we would a small child). The following practice will help you enhance your relationship with your physical form.

A meditation for receiving love through the body.

1) Start by getting comfortable. Choose a place where you can sit comfortably and reach your feet.
2) Now take your hands and begin to rub them. Notice how you feel, notice the emotions or energy rising up in you.
3) Breathe into the soles of your feet.
4) Allow it to feel like your feet are happy with you.
5) Now move up the legs to the calves and massage each calf slowly, not rushing. Enjoy it.

Practice 12 – Movement Week 1

This week we're going to start with self and body awareness and discovery. This week, every day ask yourself, "What would you like, body?" "How would you like to move?"

Take 15 minutes a day to put on some of your favorite music (meditative or not) and just move to it. Allow your body to tell you a story through your movement.

Take a few moments to jot down your experience.

Notice:

1) Where do you feel restricted?
2) Where do you feel open and strong?
3) Are you holding any excess energy and if so where?

Just take note and we will build on that in Week 2.

Practice 13 – Movement Week 2

Now that we've learned to pay attention to our bodies and hear them speak to us, we're going to begin to loosen the energetic blocks while fueling the open areas.

Look back at Week 1 and notice where you had been holding energy. This week, I invite you to breathe into those restricted areas and move them.

If it's in your heart – heart openers.

If it's in your neck – neck stretches.

If it's in your lower back – child pose and forward bends.

If it's in your feet – foot stretches.

Practice 14 – Dealing With Life Changes and Challenges

When you're going through changes and challenges, whether emotional or physical (or just in general), consider these:

1) Surround yourself not only with people who love you, but also believe in you. They must believe in the power you have to heal, the strength you have to fight and your own resolve to win this battle.

2) Don't blame yourself. This is not your fault.

3) Stay active and social. You may want to hide from the world but that won't help you get through this. By hiding away, slipping into your own precious state of depression, anxiety, or fear, and listening to your own negative talk, you can destroy your sanity and resolve to overcome your struggle. By keeping your activities and social relationships alive, you will help yourself feel normal and move through this process with a deeper sense of well-being.

4) Realize that food is a nourishment. Everything you put into your body can impact your ability to handle life's challenges – by helping or hindering it – so by seeing what you eat as natural medicine, you will become more aware of what will help fuel your body and make it able to fight whatever it is you're up against.

5) Decide and relax into the fact that it's going to be okay.

Practice 15 – Calming Stress and Grounding Into Gratitude

Feeling stressed? Frightened or panicked when possibilities start to blossom? It's critical that you learn to receive the gifts the Universe is trying to share with you (otherwise, they may stop trying!). This practice will help you to open with gratitude.

1. Sit in a chair where you can place your feet on the ground or stand.
2. Consciously give yourself permission to take five minutes.
3. Breathe deeply for four breaths in through the nose, out through the mouth.
4. Feel your feet planted on the ground, appreciating the solid floor beneath you.
5. Breathe three times allowing the solidity flooding up through your legs and into your abdomen.
6. Feel that your foundation is set, your potential is presenting itself.
7. Breathe three times and let the solidity flow up your spine, bringing strength to your back.
8. Feel your mind grow calm. You're clearing away stress.
9. Breathe three times through the back of your neck into your head, feel a blue light embracing your mind, filling your mind's eye.
10. Feel your mind opening to your inner guidance, connecting to your subconscious and spirit self. Don't think too hard, just feel open.
11. Breathe three times focusing on your forehead.
12. Breathe three times focusing on the crown of your head.
13. Breathe three times focusing on your abdomen.
14. Ask, "What is my most prosperous and passionate

project to work on right now?"

15. Breathe three times holding the question and focusing on your abdomen.
16. Hold your arms out in front of you and notice what you feel or see with your mind's eye.
17. Receive.

Remember that life is in constant motion, even when we sit in stillness, resting within our deep space of peace within. We are always manifesting and always receiving. Always expanding & retracting, observing & being, birthing & destroying. In each moment we are conscious creators and abundant receivers.

Part Three – The Spiritual Striptease

I am adrift in a cloud of bliss.

A space that is void of all reality and non-reality.

Void of any judgement of what I am, was or will be.

Surrendering to the seduction of the Cosmos I glow.

Realizing my masks and relinquishing my fears.

The world around me becomes merely a haunting of foreign sounds.

Its chatter muted by the songs of my Soul.

The music within me sings loudly,

My soul whispering knowledge and love.

Layers of Hidden Conditioning

What You'll Gain

Discover the conditionings, masks, and limiting beliefs you've been sporting as authentic versions of yourself. Begin to peel them off and become more confident in the original nature of your soul.

Hidden beneath the layers of societal definitions, cultural labels and familial traditions is your true essence. A dynamo that has been waiting for your mind to step back and allow your heart to reconnect with the truth of your being.

Unfortunately, beginning with our time in the womb, we are inundated with programs that formulate what we call our "persona", or as I like to say, "our mask". This is often the digestible aspect, the unauthentic representation that we share with the world, trusting that it fits the expectations of our communities.

Even when we break away from our trusted personalities and perhaps dip a toe into the ocean of our authentic selves, what we shine outward is most usually closer to a print instead of the original masterpiece.

We remove what makes us remarkable and create a palatable version of ourselves.

I have personally struggled with this. My parents were ministers and their views on life and reality contrasted greatly from mine since I was a child. I remember thinking that they were wrong about the existence of "the angry man in the sky watching down on us," but that it was okay, as the essence of the Universe didn't care that they believed that.

I've found myself in many destructive scenarios, some admittedly self-created and others brought on by those I love. Regardless they have left me at times internally barren and wishing for some sort of confirmation of my existence.

Believe me, if you can dance with the devil (or the darkness), I've tangoed, inviting in the darkest forms as partners and somehow believing it would deliver me to freedom.

In the end the results have been the same – me facing off with my own shadow. Nothing more, nothing less. Sometimes potent self-exploration and ruminating on what it is within me can fuel this dramatic outlook on life.

Finally, and with a sigh of relief I woke up. Not to a slice of knowledge or wisdom, but inherent understanding that the demons that I was losing myself to were merely the sides of myself I had not yet embraced. The aspects that terrified me and left me curled in a corner of my mind aching for a savior.

The irony – that savior, just as the devil, was me. Neither good nor bad but instead my expansive nature of being. The problem was my refusal to accept these very innate aspects of my being. The things that made me who I was.

I realized my own desperate thirst. It was an inner ache to be loved for all that I am, not just who I represented. This came with the searing insight that no one could ever accept me if I didn't unveil who I really was. Hiding behind a mask allowed those around me to love the mask and not the superhero behind it. However, they never truly understood the heart of the hidden being within.

What if you live your life never having been truly seen or loved? And it's simply for the reason that you never allowed anyone to see the real you, to love you.

I finally understood that love cannot be unconditional if we set conditions on ourselves. If you limit your experiences and your expressions for fear of another's trigger points, you will never find someone who can love the real you, as they won't even have the chance to know the real you.

I know… many of us are sighing at this point, believing that no one will ever make that happen. However, let's suspend disbelief and recognize that there are those out there (romantic or otherwise) that will love and understand you, but it requires that you let go of what you're settling for now. You must be open to it first.

Right now, you may only be shining at a glimmer of your full capacity. This is a mirage. It can be replaced with your innermost self solidly and confidently presenting herself to the world.

So how do we start to strip away these conditionings that muck up our authentic brilliance? By noticing and cataloging those limiting beliefs. That's the first step.

By reviewing the things we hold as truth, and taking an honest second look at them, we can begin to recognize where we may have been bamboozled into a belief that doesn't serve us. Often, we hold on to old beliefs because they make us feel safe. But what good is it to go through life lying to yourself?

Our beliefs create a framework for living, and although a certain belief structure can be productive, it can also strangle any breath of creative inspiration. All of your "dos," "don'ts," "musts," "nevers," and "shoulds" are variations of rules that box you up and create limits on the life you really want.

The constant measurement and comparison that it triggers within ourselves is even more detrimental. We are given a list of ideals to live up to, and if we fail to meet these spiritual, cultural standards it can impact how we view our self-worth.

Let's begin consciously stripping your layers away, together.

First, remove all the negativity surrounding you. I'm talking people, places, TV shows, articles, and above all the toxic echo chambers of social media. Everything you notice that's negative.

Then in the absence of all that clutter, visualize how you'd like to be, feel and react in difficult situations. At the same time, feel love and gratitude for yourself and your life every morning and every evening.

When you really start to get a feel for how you want your life to be, sink into that feeling with affirmations and mantras, such as, "I am safe in the world," or "The Universe wants me here."

Another practice I love to help shift out of old beliefs into new supportive beliefs are binaural beats combined with affirmations.

You use gamma when you're active and engaged, beta when you're concentrating, alpha when you're relaxing, theta while you're drifting off to sleep, and delta when you're in deep sleep. By shifting your internal landscape, your external landscape shifts as well, and this is a great place to start.

When we get past the muck of our old conditionings, our authentic nature may bring a sense of vulnerability or discomfort to the mind, however, it brings power to the soul. A sparkling state of joy and weightlessness takes over as we let go of the emotional baggage and the false labels we've been sporting for a lifetime.

Religion, Karma and Sin

From Childhood, many of us have had to adapt our actions to fit the families we were born into; often this was the only way we would get approval or love. Off the top of your head, can you think of times when you were young that you felt you had to hide yourself? It's probably the case that as you left your younger years and began to navigate life as an adult, those layers and masks that you had put on during childhood were still there. The way you were conditioned makes your life path less accessible. You're too busy being everything to everybody else and putting their beliefs and priorities first. That comes from living through the layers of shame, guilt and pretending.

Being raised by ministers in a home infused with religious beliefs, I had learned that certain characteristics were not just unacceptable, they were unlovable. They were allegedly a "fatal flaw within the human form."

Aspects like sexuality weren't talked about in our home. In fact, I don't recall ever having "the talk" except for when my mom told me that French kissing before being married was a sin. I've always been a sexual being, so this wasn't an easy thing for me to hear. And of course, as I grew up and began to explore and discover my sexual side, the shame that was supposed to be tied into it warred with my true self.

Like me, if you were raised in a religious home, you're most likely carrying layers of deeply rooted beliefs about yourself and the world that you may not even know you're holding onto. These may be about hell, sin, sex, guilt, shame, and self-worth.

Let's challenge these for a moment, starting with the concept of hell. If you were raised in a religious (Christian) home, you probably have a very clear image of "fire and brimstone." A place where anyone who doesn't conform to specific religious doctrine is sent to be tortured for all of eternity. This is not figurative but literal to the religious mind.

This really came to my attention when I was sitting with my sister-in-law one evening, having an eye-opening chat. She talked about her experience moving away from religious beliefs that she'd been indoctrinated with from birth. I leaned in to listen intently. She asked me, "As a mother, can you ever think of a time when your son could do something that would make you hate him enough to send him to a place where he would be tortured for the rest of his life, and never see you again? Would you alienate him?"

Of course, my first response was, "No!"

Then she said, "That's what I've realized, and it makes me believe there is no hell." She went on to explain that if there was a benevolent being that watched over mankind with love, they would, like the parent, never be able to send their kids away.

Spiritual dogma can also be rooted in old concepts such as sin. Take karma for example.

According to Hinduism, Karma teaches you that you reap what you sow, so negative actions will lead to negative outcomes, whereas positive beliefs will lead to good things in your next life. It's rather simplistic, much like how the concept of sin is that it leads to eternal damnation and death.

Sure, there's a big difference here between these two ideas, but in a certain sense, karma is sin light. There's still the basic underlying dichotomy of good versus bad equals reward versus punishment. It's a lighter version of scaring people into doing what others deem as right.

Give yourself permission and know that you're not alone.

1) It's okay to question your beliefs.
2) It's okay to question god's existence.
3) It's okay not to believe in karma.
4) Know that you're still a good person regardless of your religious beliefs.

The more we give into these outside constructs and bow down to beliefs that have been imposed upon us, the farther we step away from our authentic nature.

In the distance somewhere out there is your home and sinking into your true pool of spirit is the key to stripping off the things that weigh you down so you can fly back to your source.

Why would you want to do such a thing? Because you'll finally stop faking and start living.

If you're nodding along here, please understand, it doesn't mean there is anything wrong with you, it just means you're awakening to the work you need to do to free yourself and perform the Spiritual Striptease. This is where you get to become a maverick of your life, or as one of my favorite card decks calls it, the "Sacred Rebel". Allow that sublimely rebellious aspect out, so you turn away from those looking down at you and say, "I don't care, I love myself! And damn, I'm beautiful!"

As you begin to move through this phase, you may find that

people start to pull away from you and that life may become a bit rockier. Don't worry too much, that's simply because you're literally shaking things up. For your old conditionings to dislodge themselves, it's important for you to be willing to let go and allow yourself to grow. Sometimes you'll outgrow the old habits and people in your life. The challenge is to not go backwards or cling to those who may not see your light.

The evolution of oneself can't be forced. No matter how hard you try to fill a role or act the part, it will always remain an "Act," until you're ready. A meditation or breathing practice can really help you through the transition.

Try this: breathe in, hold, and then let it out with a full exhale through your mouth. Let your breath flood through you like a flowing river that moves through your body.

As you continue, imagine it rushing through your veins and through your lymphatic system, cleansing you, healing you, empowering you, and making you strong and fiercely confident in your authentic nature. You can chant, *I am proud of myself. I belong here, the world and Mother Nature want me here. I am healed.* A basic habit like this can serve as a powerful metaphor for the transition you're going through.

To reveal the goddess within and evolve that sensual soul can't be something our conscious mind decides to thrust upon us. The conscious mind will need to be seduced into it, so it doesn't recoil in fear. You can cultivate an internal desire to live your way into it. It can't just be the mind's choice to act it out. In fact, some change can only happen when all the vibrations of our soul self are ready to move into the shift, to claim a new pitch and create a different harmony with the reality we're existing in.

But for now, let's tie all of this together. How do you perform a spiritual striptease?

First, decide you're worthy and spend time seeing yourself for the beautiful creature you are. If you can, take a closer look at the things about yourself you want to change (not the superficial aspects, but internal shifts from deep within you).

Make that list and start becoming aware enough to make changes. Make that commitment to yourself. Learn to trust yourself – when you make promises to yourself, keep them. Look at those layers of yourself which are no longer comfortable. You can even practice this in a literal sense. Dance and you'll start to feel the sides of yourself that may be too heavy for you to move freely. Breathe through this and note. Then make a commitment to yourself to begin to remove them. Reflect on why they exist in the first place and then ask what you can do to heal or remove them. Solidify it, ask yourself if you still believe your old truths. The more you practice, the more you'll understand. Your intuition will reveal it for you.

We must unify the body, mind, and soul. That's what we'll look at in the Part on Soulphoria. Don't jump ahead! You'll miss out on all the delicious prep work.

Fears

What You'll Gain

Start recognizing the fears you've been using to hide your sublime self from your own eyes, and the eyes of the world. Recognize the layers of these false personas you wear and how good it feels to slip them off and say goodbye.

Today I heard the whispers of my doubting mind in the distance as if someone was speaking in a different language and I happened to catch it. I heard, "No one will believe in what you have to share," but even as I jot this down, I know that's not true. There will be those who doubt and judge, or don't like this perspective on the world, but that's not everyone. And so, I write for those who get it.

I've decided not to take the popular approach, made famous by the Law of Attraction, which preaches that your thoughts create your reality, so stop thinking nasty ones (or attacking yourself with them). I know how insulting and infuriating it can be to have someone say, "Just don't think about it," or "Stop focusing on negative thoughts." Of course, we would stop if we could.

Instead, I'll share a few things that have helped me push the ugly thoughts out of my head and stopped them from coming back.

Witness your worry or fear, and ask yourself, "Is this a guaranteed outcome? Is this definitely going to happen?"

For example, when I had to go back in for chemo, I was so worried that the big C wasn't gone. This fear is normal, however, it's not guaranteed to be true. In fact, it was more likely that the treatment would be effective, so by worrying about it I felt I was literally tossing away positive moments and wasting powerful energy. It's calming to take a closer look and realize your fears may have no concrete existence (unless you decide to carry them, allowing them to hitch a ride in your psyche).

Of course, there are healthy fears as well. Those are the ones that encourage you to run from a bear, or maybe to leave a party with too many people who've had a few too many drinks if a fight might be simmering. Those are our survival instinct fears. They have a place in our life and serve a purpose. That purpose is to make decisions that address them, not to obsess and fret over them. That's just the amygdala acting up when it's not needed. It's our fight or flight response.

Start by recognizing your fears, acknowledging them, and releasing them. For example, when you realize that by standing up in front of a group of people to do a talk, yes, you may be nervous, however, they won't physically hurt you. When you allow yourself to take that in, you begin to realize the fear is not rational. Ask yourself if you're in real danger, and if the answer is no, let it go.

Fear is so unfriendly. It throws nasty things at you, like insults, and that's when you know it's not healthy. Unhealthy fear will always attempt to justify itself. When you feel the fear of not being enough creeping up on you, try to witness it and relax.

As I mentioned earlier, the majority of the layers we use to cover our authentic self are fear based.

1) I'm not_____ enough.
2) I'm not as good as_____.
3) I'll never be able to_____.
4) What if I fail when I try to_____ ?

As you continue to strip away the fears that have been haunting you, you may find them calling back, like a whisper on a dark moon night, stalking you as you move among the trees. The challenge is these fears can often "make sense" and present themselves in such a way as to convince you that you're safer with them. Old fears are old friends and can give you an ironically false sense of security.

So how do you deal with these stalkers in your mind?

Change your space. When you feel the fears stalking you, go outside, move your body, literally shake them off by changing your space. This morning, when my little ogre voice rose up, I went and sat outside on the deck, watching the sun peak over the mountains and the rays bounce off the lake. Incredibly calming.

Talk to someone. But not just anyone. Someone who will be empathetic toward you without becoming a pity monster (which is not good for anyone and only adds to your gloom). Find someone who will listen, offer sound and encouraging feedback. (Someone rational.) It's also a great idea to meet people who take on brave new things themselves. They can help you prep for fearful moments. As you grow, you need to connect with a person who can grow with you, a sort of personal fear fighter superhero, who you know you can reach out to in those tough moments.

Take one step and one day at a time. You don't need to overcome all your fears in one fell swoop. Relax and tackle them bit by bit. When you break down an overwhelming fear into smaller pieces you start to see the next steps. Not only does it make it easier to handle but it also gives you small wins along the path which you can celebrate.

Write it down. Keep a diary and reflect on it. This speeds up the learning process, and allows you to objectify fears when they come up the second time around. As you step into the unknown, situations will come up that you've never dealt with before, that's inevitable. However, when you make a habit of getting calm and quiet, and sorting through everything in a journal, the risks don't seem as big. You develop confidence in your ability to handle what's ahead.

Your fears are like *The Wizard of Oz*, all you need to do is pull back the curtain and confront the little man hiding behind it.

I invite you to try something simple and unique for yourself: take a weekend for your own refueling and rebirthing. This opportunity lies not in worshipping some deity, bowing down to a god/goddess or following a set tradition, it's about refocusing your energy into your own source and feeding the energy back into your physical and spiritual forms.

Confused? Try this: Ask yourself, what would make you feel refreshed today? Would it be a quiet moment of meditation? Walking with intention? Lighting a candle for yourself? Find something to do for yourself that honors you.

Thank yourself for seeing your own worth and pulling energy inwards. Set the conscious intention that going forward you will continue to recognize this altar within yourself and spend time connecting to your own luminescent spirit, instead of kneeling to a pantheon of gods or single entity outside of your own connection to the Cosmic.

Mystic Moments

All this time I've been seeking me. Me.

Not to know who I am, but to feel alive as me.

Feel through me. Just be me without any layers of anything.

The realization that no definitions could ever fit me, for like you, I'm an ever-changing shape and a label only becomes a prison cell that we try to live within.

I may be labeled on the outside with terms like beautiful or ugly, blunt or subtle, but my internal self, my actual being cannot be captured in a web of words.

How do you define a wave when it's already changed shape before your eyes?

What you are describing is what it was. Not is.

You only express how you remember it, not the shape it holds now. And that wave is me.

To wake up from a nightmarish state and realize when intuition speaks, I feel, and know, but the mind is a loud stampede pounding the words "you must listen to me" with the desperation intuition does not have.

Intuition is awareness. Mind is fear.
Intuition is knowledge. Mind is judgement.
Intuition is flowing. Mind is analyzing.
Finally, my pieces they have healed.

And now it's forward momentum.
Creating a future.
Surfing the wave of energy, love and reality into creationism... along
the ocean of life.
Fearless, relaxed, in sync with nature. I am awake and thrilled with
the journey.

The adventure in each moment. What I am creating and the life I am
breathing.
No one can force this. So instead, I share this only to guide you
through it.
Now how do I get all this out? This immense flame of love, passion
and stories held within my system. How do I release it? It burns me
up even as I think on it. There is no logic or reason behind it, just a
desire to give it away.

I realize now that my experience was the return of pieces that
perhaps had voices to express. That a part of myself finally allowed
their grieving over elements of our past existence(s).
That finally I loved them and held them the way I chose not to before.
I loved myself. Accepted myself.
I grieved with myself and lost temper towards myself.
But in the end, it was like a lovers' quarrel and when it was through,
we were more whole than
ever before.

The Self and I.

Spiritual Hamster Wheels

Around and around we go, where we stop, only our fears will know. The spinning, twisting, whirling, of the spiritual ego. The ego can take truths and spin them around until they sound like lies.

Let's take honesty. Lies stem from the fear of telling the truth.

When someone lies, they're usually hiding a deeply buried fear of facing something about themselves, so they craft a well-thought-out story in self-preservation.

Regardless, lies are born from fear.

We know we cannot heal another person's fear. In fact, the more we coddle them and allow them to hold that fear, the more they will nourish that fear creating space for it to grow. That creates the Spiritual Hamster wheel. Rather than moving forward, so much energy is wasted sustaining the same lie.

I've often witnessed this in spiritual teachings, and I'm sure you have too, where people use their authority as a spiritual leader to spread lies and uphold old dogmas that preserve their own power.

Yet, fear is our responsibility. When you clear your own fears and blocks, you can free yourself from the teachings that would lead you astray. You can escape the hamster wheel and evolve yourself.

If you want a healthy body, your brain must communicate clearly with your cells.

It's a living breathing organism which must work as a unit.

If we want a healthy relationship, we must have honesty.

The same goes for spirituality. Foster that inner alignment and don't get caught up spinning lies to yourself. Your own or anyone else's.

When you hide the truth, you take a choice away from another being. You remove their right to make a clear decision due to your fear.

You block that person from growing with their true experiences and expanding themselves. You remove the right with your deceit. Why? Out of fear.

You don't have to untangle anybody else in order to free yourself. Any spiritual teacher can twist and turn their own agenda or cover it in wordy icing to make it sound like they know the truth. However, when you trust your inner authority, you'll be able to see through all that.

The Ghosts of Times Past

What You'll Gain

Living in the past can be compared to a drug addiction. It intoxicates us so we don't function as we could in each moment, instead we stumble along half-awake with minds full of noxious substances called dark memories. It's time to stop numbing yourself and release the ghosts stalking you from your past.

The past will continue to swarm us with emotions, like a wasp nest filled with anxious workers waiting to defend their home.

Our past can inform us through the experiences that have taught us what we know now, but they only form a skeleton or framework for our future, they don't determine it. Our brain works like an architect, constructing the future based on the past. Unfortunately, this process is primarily subconscious. However, by expanding our awareness we can get ahold of the blueprint and imagine a new framework that will allow us to build toward our desires instead of old life experiences.

The foundation of this architectural transformation is the recognition of your worth and ability to be open to desire. This is a conundrum for many of us! Desire? Allowed? What of self-sacrifice?

Moving past the cocoon stage into the place of the renewed you can be a challenge. Letting yourself be seen as your naked soul is often a scary proposition. It can cause tremors of fear to rush through you (at least it has for me).

Sometimes no amount of study of the past will bring peace. We can seek perspective, attempt to broaden our view, but it doesn't always guarantee that we won't experience pain. In reality, it's often the pain we are trying to change.

We attempt to rewrite the past to erase the discomforts hidden there, but the agony is within us. This isn't so much about the past as it's about the resentment or blame you're still carrying with you. That's what you need to let go of.

I can't promise you the pain will be gone right away, but it will no longer have a hold on you if you can stop yourself from staring at it. Don't allow the past to define you.

My past has caused me to carry a blanket of guilt, shame, and fear for years. I was traumatized by so many different events. In the beginning the grief and sorrow were relevant as they allowed me to mourn what happened. But as I moved through the years and life changed, the pain should have dissipated. Yet it didn't. Because I kept staring at it.

I allowed it to carve a long deep scar into my being that I've sported like a badge of honor. Like a warrior having been in battle.

However, there comes a point in life where you no longer want that scar. The scar becomes a distraction from living what's being offered right in front of you. We may find ourselves slipping back into old thought patterns when life's challenges come back and scare us. But that's only an excuse that gets triggered when something within us is scared to shine outwards or be accepted.

To finally be rid of this, start by fully accepting the present moment. See what's right in front of you and realize the truth of now.

But what if another person brings that past into the present? Either verbally or indirectly. Then what?

This is the challenging part of my persona for many. I don't believe in forgiveness. I believe it's a myth. It's a beautiful concept that has been fueled by the fact that it's easy to "forgive" when the person is no longer relevant. However, those who struggle and never achieve that full state of true forgiveness are ones still living with the other in their lives.

Or revenge has happened – a balancing of scales.

Right here many of you will decide to put this book down

due to the nature of this statement. Yet others will finally be able to feel better about who they are. You see – you've chased a false concept and berated yourself for not being able to be as good as those who preach this myth of being – forgiveness. I am giving you permission to realize that there is nothing wrong with you if you haven't been able to fully reach that state.

We can learn to love and still be with a person who has hurt us but that takes work. As long as you chase the concept of forgiveness it will weave, duck and spin to the side always just out of reach. Instead, live beyond the pain, out of its reach, where it's no longer a part of you. What makes it even more beautiful, this dawning day, is the knowing that nothing and no one could've rushed you. You chose sleep over wakefulness.

Now it's time to move in our power, present and awake. To be people who wish to breathe in the reality of who we are. We no longer wish to numb ourselves.

It's as if the circumference around the center was widened to give more understanding of it, clarity.

Mystic Moments

I dreamt of freedom,

of finding myself soaring over the pain,

'til I could not see it anymore.

I dreamt of lifting even higher and higher,

realizing that this river of sorrow did not come from me.

It was fed through a channel of discontent in a realm around me.

An eagle's eye view and yet also the close-up, where I can see the minute details.

Part Three Practices – The Spiritual Striptease

Practice 16 – Starting a Self-Love Affair

I'm so excited for you! You're about to embark on the greatest love affair a human can experience – one with your Soul Self!

1) If you were to wake up in the morning next to a lover/spouse/partner, you would greet them with a warm smile and a "Good Morning." Try doing this to yourself. Upon waking inwardly smile and welcome yourself to the new day.

2) Spend time getting to know the "I" within that is you. Take yourself out for coffee or relax in the park and have a chat with the inner you. Bringing along a notebook or laptop can be a great way to do this, as you can allow yourself to "free write" (meaning getting the mind out of the way and just typing whatever is coming up as you talk with yourself). It also allows you to write down key thoughts and discoveries. If you're confused about how to get started, take a deep breath, focus on an area of life or experience, and ask yourself a question (just like you would with a friend), e.g. "So, what did you truly feel about _____?" or "What's one of your dream adventures?"

3) Enjoy physical activity that makes you feel free. If you love to dance find a private room, turn on some music and seduce yourself into dancing. Ask your body to move in any way that feels fantastic and admire yourself in the process. If you like to cycle, invite yourself on a bike ride and be present, enjoying your own company while savoring the way your body feels in movement.

4) Explore what you truly look like and admire those features that stand out to you. Instead of rushing through doing your makeup or brushing your hair as you hurry

to get dressed, try actually seeing yourself in the mirror. Get to know your face, your eyes, your body – appreciate what you see and allow yourself to be proud of it.

5) Make Love to Yourself. Loving yourself physically as well as emotionally is a powerful way to enhance your self-worth while connecting more genuinely into your sexual self. Even by merely caressing your own skin, running your hands over your thighs or delving further into the realm of self-seduction and experiencing how much pleasure you can bring to yourself; a shift will happen in your system that will create ripple effects in all parts of your life.

Practice 17 – Stripping the Layers Spiritually

Let's begin consciously stripping your layers away.

1) Remove the negativity surrounding you. Detox yourself of any people, places, TV shows or articles that drag you down and keep you small.

2) Visualize how you'd like to be, feel and respond to difficult situations.

3) Feel love and gratitude for yourself and life. Every morning and every evening.

4) Say an affirmation – "I am safe in the world. The Universe wants me here."

5) Use Binaural Beats combined with those affirmations.

   a) Gamma when you're active and engaged.

   b) Beta when you're conscious and actively concentrating.

   c) Alpha when you're relaxing.

   d) Theta when you're drowsy or lightly sleeping.

   e) Delta when you're in deep sleep.

By reviewing the things we hold as truths and honestly looking at them, we can begin to recognize where we may have been bamboozled into a belief. Understand that for many people their beliefs help them to feel safe, but what good is feeling safe if ultimately you're lying to yourself?

Practice 18 – Inventorying Your Beliefs

Getting Started on Exploring your Beliefs:

1) Make a list of your foundational views. For instance, do you believe in a God? Do you believe in reincarnation? Do you believe in sin?

2) Now take a step back, choose one and dive in. When did this belief start? Watch out for those beliefs that you've had since childhood. Was this belief born of an experience you've personally had or one you've been taught? Be open. If you find yourself shutting down here, you may have touched on a belief you need to explore. Question the validity of this belief. What makes it a truth for you, based on what evidence? Resistance and doubt often shine a light on those areas where we've adopted blind faith, which is most often embedded within us from others.

Practice 19 – Letting Go of Un-serving Beliefs

1. Stop for a moment and think of a spiritual, religious, or new age practice you're currently using, or have used in the past.

2. Ask yourself, "What's a guideline, rule or viewpoint that this tradition holds that I don't always follow?"

3. Remember a time when you broke one of these rules and how it felt. Did you beat yourself up for it?

4. Now ask yourself, "What is my truth around this rule?" Do I truly feel in my source that this is something that helps me live a more blissed-out life or is it in some way stopping me from expressing myself, taking chances or making changes?

When we begin to investigate the boxes we've adopted to confine ourselves, we will find that these tiny spaces don't allow for forward movement. They create a restrictive channel of flow, expecting you to choose one road and stay there.

Part Four – The Sublimely Naked Soul

I dance sublimely naked with my spirit.

My thoughts stripped from me like clothing.

My labels vanishing, definitions dissolving.

I find myself empty and within this I am full.

So full I cry out as my Spirit caresses my mind

... and asks me to never cover it again.

The Exhibitionistic Spirit

What You'll Gain

Once you've shed the layers of the past, you'll start to find your new comfort zone. We're going to build upon that sensational foundation of self-knowing, lean on that cosmic cheering squad and discover what sorts of shimmy our spirit likes to do as she glides through this life. We are readying ourselves to make waves out into the world. By the end of this chapter, you will be on your way to becoming one magnetic female who is ready to say yes to the tango of life.

Shhh... can you hear that? In the distance there is a cosmic beat playing softly. A sacred musician pouring his passion onto the skins of a spiritual drum. He glances up and we are caught in his gaze. He plays for us. He plays for you. He is the cosmic drummer come to embrace your soul with music so sensual, so strong that you begin to move and sway. Your hips finding their unique way to express the beat... and slowly... calmly... you begin to strip. Allowing the layers of fears to drop to the floor, you undo the clasps of conditionings and let them drift off on the wind. Finally reaching up, your hands grasp hold of the mask you've been wearing... and you allow it to drop.

A swell of emotion fills the space as your guides savor the sight of your Soul. The universe cheers for the beauty of your undressed, undefined self and you; for the first time in life your mind realizes how incredibly radiant, sexy, and powerful you are.

Often one of the most terrifying concepts to the mind is "being truly seen" not for the persona we've so diligently crafted to manipulate the minds of those around us, but to be witnessed in that sublimely naked form.

We're told it takes courage to step out of our labels, fearlessness and perhaps a touch of what could be termed healthy insanity, but in reality, the true key is the unconditional love for what we are.

Remember that love affair with the self that we started? Now it's time to share that radiance we discovered with the world. I keep telling you the world is waiting and now it's time to shake that sexy spiritual booty and get ready to groove on the earthly dance floor.

During this portion of your journey, you'll be making space in your life for new opportunities and people to flow in. There's a tendency for us to want to fill up empty spaces immediately, but no worries, we'll be working on tending the open spaces and allowing the breath of life to move through them. Bringing with them new ways of being, from new hobbies to new foods to a new life.

Your soul didn't come all the way down here to sit and stare in a mirror. It came to live, breathe, dance, taste, and experience. It came here to teach, love, and share. The point is it came to live through this body, engaging and weaving its energy in the world around it.

Our system is actually quite delicate. It's easily impacted by the environment we choose to exist within, and even more so, the things we decide to take in. Not just food but entertainment, conversations, activities and even thought processes.

One night I was lying in bed thinking about my day, and a strange switch flipped within me. Suddenly it was as if I began to see the mirror reflection of every thought I had. As if for the first time I saw the flipside of the coin. I don't mean in the lives of others, I mean for myself and my own choices.

I saw certain ways I may spend my time – such as reading bad news or gossip with unhealthy plotlines. I'd know it wasn't serving me, and yet, I'd keep doing it. If something creates this sort of ugliness within us and spreads out to how we engage with others throughout our day, why would we continue doing it? Because we haven't realized the impact it has on the big picture.

Newton's third law of motion states that every action has an equal and opposite reaction. Every activity, no matter how small it seems, will impact your energetic system either in a miniscule or infinite way. The true mystery of this is you may not always be aware of where your reaction comes from, until you become more conscious of it. You may feel that that upset from earlier was due to what the person said to you, when in fact it was that book you decided to pick up before you left for work or that news piece that took up space in your system, tripping up old fears that you have hidden and not healed. We are a mysterious, web of experiences until we take the time to recognize them and sort through the tangle.

The first step is to listen within.

The second is to be open to your truth, fearlessly. Your truth is those things that trigger you that you'd love to deny. They're often little secrets that you haven't yet admitted to yourself.

The third is to go deeper into listening within, to witnessing lovingly yourself in various moments. When you address the trigger with love, it will uncover itself for you.

The fourth is to end your day with a recap from above, watching the truth of your reactions, choices, and interactions. Take some time to reflect.

The fifth is the detox.
This can be such a rejuvenating experience for your spirit that it gives me chills just thinking about it!

It's not easy remaining naked in your soul self, and often we'll find ourselves reverting to old habits. Don't be afraid to stand up for yourself. This is important and has the potential for profound transformation from the inside out.

Client's Story

When I was hosting a spiritual retreat for some of my clients, Lisa had been having challenges standing up for herself and being able to really speak her mind. As a yoga teacher she'd worked with various holistic schools of thought, from yoga therapy to chakra work, to release this block.

As she performed the spiritual detox and meditation during one of our workshops, she witnessed her teen self split in two. One side of her younger self had so much to say and share, often differing from opinions of others, however, the other teenage side wanted to keep things harmonious and was scared of the fighting and repercussions that would happen with family if she spoke her mind. In the end that teenager was muffled and prevented from expressing her true voice.

The younger teenager was a peacemaker at any cost, but the grown woman became angrier and angrier. When Lisa asked what she could do to release the fears, her father (who had passed) came up and started shouting at her, putting her down. Finally, the teenager began to express herself, standing up to her father. The father left, and Lisa and her teen side embraced. Lisa then made a promise to her teenage self to protect the younger voice while still being true to the woman she'd become. She finally understood why the block had existed and from then on began to create healthy boundaries and true self-expression.

Spiritual Detox

What You'll Gain

Reveal those hidden pollutants that seem benign and perhaps even helpful. Even spirituality can be polluting if it's not coming from the right place. So, let's discover how it may be clouding your view and causing a fog in your intuition.

We often think of our personal opinions and viewpoints being infiltrated by the fog of media which surrounds us in daily life: television, radio, advertising, magazines. Knowing how these can shade our perspectives, many have taken to clearing out their minds on a regular basis. I call this a detox.

Yet when it comes to the world of spirituality, we may never take the time to give ourselves space and gain clarity.

Religions and traditions can limit our perspectives and experiences. They can even become a sort of pollution for the soul. Their very nature is limited, with each one offering a set of rules: do, do not, must not, should not. This framework restricts the inner artist of the soul self, the creative being within and the ability to uncover our true nature. Instead, life becomes about how well you live within the constructs of these strict rules, how disciplined you are and how well you sacrifice.

There is no medal at the end of this road.

Many of the old traditions taint the elements that make up our lives as lesser than. The body, the mind, the world around us are like a stain on the soul, instead of a vehicle for discovery. This creates a feeling of guilt just by being, shame just by feeling, struggle simply by living.

New adages have arisen to persuade us that the perfected existence resides outside of this realm and that "one day" you will get there. Now ask yourself, if we live with the concept that "one day" things will be better, that "when we die" we'll go to heaven, then we will move through life never satisfied. These spiritual traditions perpetuate a negative viewpoint on life and plant a seed that creates perpetual discontentment.

Accepting a tradition and adopting it as yours binds you to your raw inner wisdom.

Yes, there are amazing aspects to many of these philosophies and mythologies, but to blindly embrace them as a truth is to live a life of self-inflicted imprisonment. As a result, we carry tension, struggle, a constant seeking for something "more" yet also the judgement of the self for being unsatisfied with your chosen path.

The Spiritual Detox is an opportunity to clear all of that out. Here are some basic guidelines to help you get started.

Media Detox

Take a weeklong break from all spiritual stimulants. No books, no spiritual teachers, no podcasts, no apps, no blogs, or articles... no nothing. (Was that a gasp?) This detox will help to cleanse your palate and clear the clutter that's been placed there by various media. Then you'll have more space for your own personal inquiry. In the end it'll aid you in exploring and reclaiming your own spiritual ecosystem, which may have been rented out to your favorite spiritual pundits, yoga sites or mystic publications. You'll be surprised by how light you can feel after being bogged down by the influx of religious materials.

Your Beliefs

Make a list of your biggest truths/falsehoods. Once you get to the ones that make you squirm (for example, "I don't believe there is a god" is a common truth that people are afraid to question, or "I don't believe in Karma"), keep going. When you reach those that have you thinking, "I can't write that down," keep going.

When you finally touch upon those that make you question yourself (and may have you denying fervently that "These can't be my beliefs!") then you've arrived. Now rip up that list (or even better, burn it – safely that is) and with each tear of the paper or wisp of flame, feel yourself letting them go. All of them. Trust that you're a beautiful being without them and you don't need them. Once you've done that sit with yourself and meditate on just being.

Savoring the Reality Around Us

Enjoy the dynamic array of life around you in the world from nature to people. During your weeklong break from spiritual lectures, online meditation, and deep reading (yes even from this book!) notice what draws your attention. Listen to your intuition. Listen to your body. Feel your mind and be present with the truth that is you. Note down any interesting insights or thoughts that come up. You may be surprised at what pulls you in (spiritual or non-spiritual), and you may even be shocked at the depths of your own insights.

Your Personal Fantasy Land

Take a few breaths and let your mind wander. Let the perfect time and place unfold in your mental theater. It may be imaginary, off planet, from current or past life, it doesn't matter. Just free yourself to allow yourself to rest in this space.

Although mass-produced spirituality can bring some interesting new ideas to our internal landscapes, it can also overtake our own authentic voices and knowledge. When you let go of others' ideas and rediscover your own, you'll regain a more stunning connection with yourself. You'll embrace your unique soul in a new way, and to top it off you may discover the most mind-blowing Soulphoric experience you have ever had. Why? Because it comes from the depths within you, from those things that don't simply turn on your mind or body, but your entire being.

Adventures in Soul Shout Outs

What You'll Gain

The following is to give you a taste of my experience and proud soul shout outs. As I went through the period of becoming a proud Soul exhibiting herself in daily life, I hit many challenges and a few "friendly" roadblocks with those who loved me yet feared what I was morphing into. You see, as our divine voices grow louder, they give off a higher vibration that may not be music to the ears of those around us. In fact, it may scare them. Don't be surprised if it has some of your friends hiding under a blanket of "normal" and hoping to tug you under with them.

Excerpt from my Blog 2011:

I'm smiling as I type this... with a bit of mischief in my eyes and my shadow side proudly holding the hand of my light aspects... the entire me is sitting here beaming out at you... I feel fulfilled. Do you know why? Because I'm not editing myself right now.
I've fired my internal "Editor." Bid Adieu to my "Political Correctness Checker" and told my "Internal Producer" to step aside, my Soul is taking charge.

This body, this mind, this life experience is now under the management of its original owner... my Spirit. And damn does it feel good!

The funny thing is, the more I live this and allow my entire self to reign, to shine out into the world everywhere I go, the more I'm hearing a common sentiment: "I can't believe you did that" or (and picture this one accompanied by a slightly worried expression...) "Haha... you're not really going to do that... are you?"

The thing is the worry they're feeling is not real and their fear has no relation to my safety or sanity. It's all ego based. Let me rephrase what my friends and colleagues (and I sincerely know they are trying to be loving) are really saying: "What will (fill in the blank) think?!" "Imagine what (fill in the blank) will say?"

Now before I continue, let me explain something very important here. I know many of you are currently nodding your head along with my message. Feeling what I'm saying and probably cheering it on with a "rock your authenticity, girl!" and thank you! But there is something important you should be aware of here, when I say I fired my internal editor – "I fucking mean it!"

My friends and colleagues are not just dealing with someone who has decided to be a "good spiritual authentic Chiquita," willing to demonstrate her spirituality by meditating in public, or perhaps fearlessly discussing past lives in front of others, using terms like spirit guides regardless of who's around. No...

I'm talking about authentically going around spiritually naked in public. Proudly strutting down a busy street as a sublime Spirit who is high on the human experience and fascinated by the world around. Your soul is proud of her whole self, and that includes her shadow side as much as her light. She doesn't withhold her love from different sides of herself because some archaic tradition or religion says, "that aspect is dark." She loves truly her entire being.

I love my sexuality. I am kinky as hell in the rawest ways. I've loved men and women (sometimes at the same time) and I'm proud of it. My love knows no bounds and sees no gender, so why should that make others cringe?

I love to dress up. My body is a temple and one I love to wrap myself in whatever my soul feels like in that moment, using my clothing as a fun expression of who I am. From stiletto heels, short dresses to long skirts and scarves... I dress never to impress but to express.

I love recreational supplements. I have no addictions and truly feel for those haunted by that constant need. I've seen it, witnessed the damage and supported others through that journey. Yet authentically I enjoy savoring a glass of red wine. My Spirit gets excited at the thought of shamanic journeying with the aid of Peyote and I do believe that "green herbal goodness" should be legalized.

I love meat. My body craves it, my taste buds tingle with it, and even though I've tried the vegetarian route, after three years it didn't work. Some spiritual folks will look at me with a slight disdain thinking that a truly enlightened being would be vegan, while I smile back at them and think a truly enlightened being would never judge.

I love to dance. I can dance till four in the morning, feeling my energy caress my body to the beat of the drums, my spirit shouting, "Oh yeah!" as it experiences the freedom of this form moving in rhythm to the magic produced by the DJ, celebrating this life experience with all the other souls in the room lost in bliss.

I love myself completely, every nook and cranny. I celebrate this life experience, living as a spiritual hedonist, meaning I live each moment through the senses of the Spirit.

So, backing up to my friends and their recent repetitive shock at my willingness to expose my true authentic self, to say what I mean with strength, to demonstrate my truth with pride and to live this life with fierce soul-filled love. I thank them for their care and worry, but I let them know there's no need. This is who I'm meant to be and what I'm meant to do in the world.

Your Spirit is in charge now. Although what you do and express may shock people and boggle minds as it defies the conditions to which we've all become accustomed to. But don't worry. Let go of all of the concerns, the grasping for the old, conditioned responses, and even the traditional religious and/ or spiritual ways of doing things. It's not about the outside world. It's about us, women, loving ourselves enough to set our souls free.

It's time for you to join me in turning this life experience into a blissed-out, self-discovering spiritual safari with no judgements toward your true desires and dreams. No more labeling your shadows and demons, but rather embracing all you're realizing: that your spirit IS the child, the sexy diva and the goddess. How about it? Let's become exhibitionistic souls.

The Essence of Confidence

True confidence lays beyond the actions you take and instead ignites from the womb. Many people will fake confidence, because they're trying to be what they consider sexy, or stylish, or rebellious but true confidence comes from within you. It comes from loving yourself and enjoying so many savory moments. With a healthy kind of selfishness, take what you need to feel self-assured or at least ask for it. This is because you've experienced how good your body, mind and soul feel when you do your best. This is not about asserting the ego, trying to feel superior, or harm anyone in any way. It's about the love, health, beauty and light in all things.

Releasing Your Cultural Identities (and being okay with it)

My blood flows with many colors, a spectrum of races. Literally. Kissed by African blood, intertwined with Turkish and a blend of some sort of European yet unknown to me. And yet mine is hidden in amongst shadows. I find myself wandering between the shade, as our society calls for a declaration of who you are.

What's your culture? Your birth? How does it play into your identity?

When I'm confronted with this question, instead of reaching for the explanation of Turkish, African and English (and being greeted by a confused look), I've adopted the global residence approach. Confounded individuals would attempt to place me into their boundaries, however, I am all and none. I'm adopted with no ties to anything and yet tied by blood to many. In the end, aren't we all?

I've finally surrendered to not standing for one thing, realizing that in the end it doesn't matter. The love of those around me and the experience of joy is the only thing that fuels me. At the end of the day any other philosophy is empty of meaning. All the other formulas for happiness can be studied and dissected, but ultimately torn apart.

Fears of Not Being Seen

Being seen can get in the way of being who you are.

People chase after status, titles and even photographs in the society papers. They believe it will somehow give purpose to their existence, when in reality it only distracts from their reason for being. Any superficial definitions drain our mysticism and reduce us to one of the herd (albeit perhaps a glossier member).

In fact, it's a fear of not being seen, for if they are not seen, not recognized, not labeled, they are left as nothing. Standing on weak knees which don't know how to hold them up without the props of the world around. But love of the deepest kind remains, no matter how far we run or where we hide.

Are we all seeking definition when there is none that actually fits? A cloak we hope that will fit, but in some way needs tailoring. In the end we're merely the earth animated by the kiss of something unknown. Maintain your Sublimely Naked Soul (with Pride!).

Mystic Moments

I used to seek a name. A place. Somewhere to belong.

Now I know that I only belong to the being that animates me.

Whatever that is. I claim to know. Yet know nothing I admit.

In this admission, there is such joy.

To embrace all and celebrate every culture that runs through the veins and of those that surround me.

To celebrate not the upbringing that has formed me, but the creature that resides within.

The wild nature we all hold within.

It stirs me in a way that nothing can.

Other People's Reactions to Your Nudity

What You'll Gain

Moving past the change stage into the place of the renewed you can be a challenge. Letting yourself be seen in your naked soul is often a scary proposition. It can cause tremors of fear to rush through you (at least it has for me).

Change within us can cause others to recoil. The key is to remain in your strength and understand a negative reaction to your evolution is about the other person, not you. Most often this happens when the person feels you're reflecting back to them and what they wish they could do. You're making those around you potentially aware of the changes they'd like to make. They may throw it back to you with phrasing such as, "I don't know who you areanymore."

It's okay if this happens. It's certainly happened to me. As you shift through the many layers of yourself stripping away the masks, you may also notice that your relationships change. Over the last 10 years I've experienced some of the biggest and yet most bountiful shifts in my life.

I left a marriage and found myself.

I lost close friends and opened to new family.

I dumped definitions and fell in love with my no labels, no veils sublimely naked spirit.

I've beaten a disease and reclaimed divine health.

And in the end I came home, to me.

Through this experience of floating in a sea of change and learning to not attempt to swim against the current of the cosmos, one of the biggest personal challenges you may experience is the shifting of friendships. I'm sure you've been taught that love comes and goes, with lovers making grand entrances through the front door and slipping out or being kindly asked to exit through the side door.

Yet somehow, we may feel that we're entitled to certain friendships forever, even though most of us haven't spoken to our high school "posse" for years and that once-closest confidant may no longer be listed in our e-mail contacts. When they don't, the disappointment can be more overwhelming than that of a lost lover.

Hmm... Interesting isn't it? A friendship is still an engagement of sharing, giving, receiving, and inspiring through interaction, just like with a partner. Therefore, just like a relationship, it's important to be able to stand strong without it, yet always appreciate, nourish, and cherish it while we have it.

Just as with partners, friendships can shift. They may change from negative and confusing situations to mutual understanding or take another turn and simply a drifting apart.

As you begin to experience transformations, many of your friendships may change too. Some of them will start to fade. You may find yourself wondering what it was that had caused these departures. Take a deep breath and know that you have embarked on such a different voyage from those around you, that your choices may no longer make sense to them. Who you're becoming was not who they believed they had invested their "friendship energy" into and thus they no longer feel they know you.

On the other hand, your friends might be wondering how to keep up, or how to connect with the new you. They may even wonder if the new you still knows and still loves them. The truth is, there's a decision to be made here. You can walk up to them and say, "Hello, my name is (fill in the blank), let's get to know each other again."

However, for most people that's not an easy option. Change seems to threaten the comfort zone of most people. Especially when it's someone very close to them who has shifted, it can cause their own foundation to feel shaky.

For some your change can also be a reflection back of their

own unlived dreams, their fears of "going for it" whatever "it" is to them, or feeling that they are lacking in their own personal growth. Regardless of what they are experiencing, this can cause a longtime friend to pull away.

What I've learned is to allow friends to float back into the open sea. Don't cling, don't struggle trying to pull back their anchor and park them next to you. Let them go and say, "Thanks for stopping by in this life! Your company was appreciated, your love savored and perhaps we'll meet again."

As your old friendships shift, you're making room for amazing new connections in your life. You'll open yourself up to meeting new people that inspire and nourish the new life you're exploring. It's beautiful to me how when we make space in our lives, a stunning abundance of things, people and experiences enter.

Although I don't place any expectations for these new relationships, I do appreciate them standing strong next to me in the moments we share. I'm open to those moments lasting forever or a day.

Today, love yourself enough to say goodbye to those friends who don't know how to love you back.

Embrace that even an experience that seems to degrade your spirit and challenge the mind is merely a temporary test. You can step up and above the current plane you exist upon and imagine something greater.

For each tear I've shed, I realize I'm stronger. This doesn't mean I shut myself down and turn off from the experiences that life can and will bring me. I've discovered an indefinite well of power within me.

That same well resides deep within you. Do you know where it is? Do you recognize how it feels? Can you feel it shift and evolve as you go through each experience? Like the cells of your body you constantly shed, it evolves, and it rejuvenates your entire being. It's your life force.

I'm wiser.
I'm stronger.
My perspective is broader.
I see more.
I'm alive in each breath.
It's what your essence sees that your eyes are blind to.
What your mind may not be able to process at this moment.
But later will look back upon and say, "I finally see."

Integrity in the Self

What You'll Gain

Now that we've created all this space for the new, it's time to pull down your universal power. This is your natural energy that will fuel your confidence and your transformation.

Integrity is an anchor into our authentic self, the sublimely naked soul. When we work from a place of integrity, we learn to express our truth and to keep our word to ourselves and to others. I experienced this for myself when I returned to work full-time after the big C Experience. I had the opportunity to pick up a project I had been working with previously, which would've been potentially great income and a good opportunity. And yet I felt this was out of sync with who I had become. This happens a lot once we've gone through a transformative experience. We can't fit back into the boxes we placed ourselves in before. So, coming from a place of integrity, I stepped away strongly.

As you blossom fully into your sublimely naked soul, you discover what you'd like for yourself and your life. You feel it quite intensely. And you'll learn how and when to say no to those things that don't serve your purpose and being. As you step more into your integrity you'll naturally start to draw in people and opportunities that feed you, providing you the nourishment you require to evolve on your path. Don't be frightened by this. Make the leap.

Consider that while you step further into integrity it's important to embrace your new choices. You must believe in your decision, and not question yourself. Make your decision, set your intention, and then get out of the way. Working from a place of integrity will bring you a renewed sense of confidence and self-worth. You'll naturally be attracted to those things that are best for you in this life. Once again, remember, to receive these we must be willing to let go of those things and people that now no longer fit.

This is my body.

I love my body.

My body, mind and heart are united, all one.

I am one.

I am.

The evolution of oneself can't be forced, no matter how hard you try to fill a role or act the part. That's all it is and will remain an "act" until you're ready.

Regardless of the gateway that has brought you here, we all have one thing in common, one lesson that must be learned and embraced if we are to move forward and dive deeper. That is the understanding and discernment of the soul. Embrace this adventure.

What brings you bliss?

What You'll Gain

Here we're going to have some fun, engaging the courage to follow your passion. You express your soul self by prioritizing the activities that bring you joy. This takes courage, but once you start, you'll never look back.

I can't emphasize the importance of spending time doing what brings you closer to your soul self enough. This means finding passions and following them. Whether it's writing, painting, dancing or skydiving. Do it. Engage in play and express your spirit's voice, otherwise we become buried in the mundane which leads to disassociation with our inner being. We become depressed with living.

Finding and expressing your true voice doesn't always mean literal vocalization, it may be simply a walk on the beach, connecting with the warmth that being close to water raises within you.

Or perhaps you love to move your body in sync with your spirit. Then do it. Take time to listen to a song that resonates inwards (no, this doesn't have to be some sacred tune or monks chanting, it can be dance music). Find something that makes you want to relax, and free yourself to soar to the beat and then glide back, deep into the earth. Move with the goddess hidden there. The key is to let go. Liberate yourself through these activities and in becoming closer and closer to the true you.

I've nicknamed this "dating myself" because it truly is a love affair with your spirit. Every time you do this you build a deeper bond, and the spirit emerges as the creator and guide within this life's journey. When you put the soul self first, this allows the mind to step back into the role of interpreter and the body to celebrate being savored for the job it's doing.

When I don't write I begin to lose myself, feeling a sense of emotional sadness seep into my days. I wonder what's happened to cause such despair, and then I remember. My soul is calling.

Try this, ask yourself what you'd like to be doing right now? Is your body, heart, or soul nudging you toward something? If so, go do it! Right now! I'll be waiting for you in between these pages until you return.

The days I create, I write, I dance, and do rituals – I glow! I feel more alive, and the energies of both confidence and courage fill me. There have been days spent creating, like the one in which I'm writing this book. I feel that I'm once again a teenager and have stumbled upon some forbidden party that I'm welcomed into. Forbidden – why? Because it feels too good to be normal, but it is.

In our society, we've succumbed to the mundane. We're so detached yet thrust into a workforce that expects us to engage, that we numb ourselves to be able to survive.

I know, I've been there.

The only way to truly break this cycle is by creating a renewed and solid relationship with your authentic self. One that is not fleeting but takes action in the direction of our dreams. That creates such intense draw and curiosity about who you are and what you're passionate about.

It's time for a self-love affair. It's one of the greatest gifts you can give yourself, for it will truly change your state and ripple joy from your inner self out into the world around.

Now, let's kindle a few ways to start this love affair.

Life is Beautiful Chaos

What You'll Gain

When you notice chaos starting to reveal herself, you're in the prime place to reposition the pieces of your life into what would be a masterpiece. For only when things seem to crumble and dissolve, do we have the opportunity to brush away the rubble (whether physical, emotional or mental) and rebuild on a clear foundation.

Chaos provides us with the opportunity to passionately take an interest in our soul evolution. We can look upon this life as an epic spiritual odyssey and step up to navigate this adventure instead of remaining a passive passenger.

The hidden secret is to see yourself as something worth exploring with your consciousness. Realize that you, yourself, are worth the investment that you put into other areas, such as work, family, or friends. The energy, love, and loyalty you give to others is exactly what your soul is hoping you will also give to yourself.

Through this practice you become fascinated with who you are, and along the way you become more forgiving toward what you perceive are your mistakes. You become passionate for your life path. You learn to dance with chaos, realizing that it's merely a tool for change.

What a wonder it is when we finally surrender.

It's time for you to go out into the world and be proud of who you are. How do you shine? What are your colors?

I know how hard it can be to let go and trust ourselves.

After my first clear MRI, it was a challenge for me to let go of my identity with the big C. If I'm honest, it's only been a week since I received my positive results, so I'm talking to you from the space of trying to let go. It's interesting how traumatic events happen to us in life and we somehow identify with them, long past the actual event.

The challenge is to stop labeling yourself with the negative circumstance. Reframe your language around it. For example, let's say you've hurt your back, so you go through life saying, "I have a bad back." Well, that's never going to change if you keep telling yourself that's how it is or that's who you are.

The Renaming

Let go of your past stories. Don't reach back and retell them out of a sense of security. Allow your labels to fall away like a silk robe sliding off your shoulders. You may feel lost at first, when you're no longer anchored to that story from the past. Still, don't cling. Instead, be in the moment and flow with it. Let your body and soul lead you. Find out who you are now.

If you find yourself still being pulled back, try working out, doing yoga, meditation, qi gong, or anything that will change your physical space, inward and outward. This will help you to cleanse the energy body.

Today I'm working to create more space between my past and my present self. Not to lose the lessons and experiences I had but instead feel comfortable in my new skin.

Too often we focus on the negative experiences as lessons, and completely forget about the positive ones. Today, I encourage you to make a list of positive experiences that turned out to be lessons. Feel the support you've received from those positive lessons. Embrace the feeling of being held by the Universe.

Mystic Moments

Life has been rushing by in a blur of deep colors,
sweeping me up in its embrace like the wind.
Carrying me forward on the breeze.
And depositing me back on the banks of the earth.

In all of this I've danced with Chaos, smiling at its hidden beauty
and recognizing the wonder of change.

For Chaos is the parent of metamorphosis.
It brings transformation.

Part Four Practices – The Sublimely Naked Soul

Practice 20 – Finding Your Soul Spark

An Energy Breathing Exercise – this exercise is a great way to kick off your day and add a boost of energy to your body! It is also key to finding the "Soul Spark" within you!

Usage: Daily

Time: AM

Length: approx. 5-10 minutes

1) Find a quiet space where you will not be disturbed. You can do this exercise:
   - In the Shower
   - Outdoors (in nature)

   (Please never attempt while driving, operating heavy machinery, or riding unicorns.)

2) Calm yourself with a few deep breaths, feeling yourself grounded and centered.

3) Ask within, "Where is the seat of my Soul this morning? Where is my Divine Spark within me?"
   You will feel a tingling, awareness or cognitive knowing. Wherever it is, bring your conscious awareness there (you may also wish to place your hands on that part of your body to bring a physical connection).

4) Say to your mind, "Step back, relax and do not interfere or analyze, merely witness.".

5) Breathing and connect with the Spark – feel as if you're breathing into it.

6) Take three deep relaxed breaths focusing on connecting

with that Spark within.

7) Allow any visuals to form, experience any feelings or knowing without analysis.

You may experience emotions, insights, colors, images... relax and allow.

Practice 21 – Kindle Your Soul

Breathing as a Bellow to kindle the flame of your Soul Spark.

1) Inhale a short breath and release through your nose a quick forced exhale (using your abdomen muscles).
2) Repeat up to five times or until you feel that spark has grown.
3) Take three relaxed breaths with full awareness on your Soul Flame, love it, know it.

Practice 22 – Connecting With Your Soul Spark

Breathing to Open and Merge with the Soul. This practice will enable you to connect into your Soul, empowering and embracing it!

1) Take two relaxed breaths feeling your entire system opening to merge with your Soul.

2) Bringing your awareness back to the flame you are now ready to breathe the Soul fire into your entire physical self, mind, and energy body.

   a. Step breaths – short inhale (no exhale) followed by another short inhale that brings the breath up through your body and end with a slow soothing exhale.

   b. Repeat the step breath three times knowing that each inhale opens a floodgate for the Soul fire to fill your entire system and each exhale allows you to sink deeper into the merging of your Soul Self and Human Experience.

3) Opening to Constant Awareness and Insights – take three relaxed breaths and affirm, "I am whole, awake and aware."

Practice 23 – Ground into Your Power Center

This exercise will empower you, bringing in the power of the Universe down through your upper chakras, focusing on spirituality and the mind, and drop that energy down into the base of the spine, the root chakra or the "I am" center. Here you can allow Universal energy to pool at the foundation of your energy system and nurture you. You're also claiming your body.

You can use this exercise to fully incarnate your power in this life. By doing this you're solidifying your energy and empowering it to take your ideas and make them real. The descending power is great for those who feel awakened in their upper energy points (intellect, creativity, spirituality).

Let your breath flood through you like a river moving through your body. Feel your veins transmitting your energy through your lymphatic system, cleansing you, healing you, empowering you, and making you strong. Feel the energy embrace you, honoring you, worshipping you. Allow that to soak into your heart and ignite the fiercely confident power of your authentic nature.

Say to yourself:

I am proud of myself. I belong here, the world and Mother Nature want me here. I am healed.

Practice 24 – Honoring Yourself

Take time to invest back into your source, recognizing the God/ Goddess within (or the "Divine I").

Ask yourself, what would make you feel refreshed today? Would it be a quiet moment of meditation? Walking with intention? Lighting a candle for yourself?

Thank yourself for seeing your own worth and pulling that energy inwards.

Set the conscious intention that going forward you will continue to recognize the altar within yourself and spend time connecting to your own luminescent Spirit self.

Part Five – Becoming a Mistress of Mysticism

You've seen her,

that woman who walks in a room and there's just

something about her.

She has a fascinating aura of mystery, awe, and power surrounding her.

She radiates sensuality, confidence in her sexuality and

a definitive connection to the feminine mystery.

She is an exhibitionistic Spirit, proud of her naked Soul.

She knows no need for labels

for she has savored the seduction of the Cosmos.

Dancing with Your Feminine Side

What You'll Gain

To be able to step fully into your power, you must be able to embrace yourself. That includes the feminine aspects of yourself which make up your own unique goddess.

Let's start by playing a simple game. I'm going to give you a set of words and I want you to notice whatever you picture in your mind.

Feminine energy.

Feminine magic.

Goddess.

In our world we have been taught that the feminine equates to women.

To unite our energy internally for Soulphoria we need to heal our relationship to the feminine. That means beginning to embrace being female. This is where we embrace the form we've decided to encompass in this life.

Even in our traditions, cultures, or Eastern/Western religious philosophies the Goddess is always shown as a fully-grown woman. The goddess is never a child, yet the child is just as much female as the woman.

Why is this?

When you were a little girl, were you any less feminine?

When you were a teenager, were you any less feminine?

Now that you're a woman, are you more feminine?

Remember I'm not asking if you compare yourself on the spectrum of society's normal view of what is "feminine." No. I'm simply asking you if you're more female.

It seems so simple, doesn't it?

Yet somehow, we've lost the concept that the feminine energy encompasses all aspects of our life experience. To be fully connected to that dynamic radiant energy, we must in fact embrace all personas of the female self within, starting with the child, the teen, and the woman.

The most common imagery that comes up with feminine energy and the Goddess is one of an adult woman. Perhaps you relate this to the Venus, Aphrodite, Athena, Lakshmi, Saraswati or Kali. Each of these were adult, female Goddesses.

Now, let's go back to the earlier reflection. How many of you thought of a child when I said, "feminine energy"? How many of you thought of a teenager?

Most likely, very few people did, if any. This is because we usually relate Goddesses and/or feminine energy to womanhood. Which leaves us missing out on invaluable aspects of ourselves (the child and the teen) when we embark on the adventure of healing and journeying into wholeness in ourselves and our feminine power.

The feminine energy flows through your entire life, from conception until death. This means it draws on every stage, including the child, which is sadly so often left out of the Goddess equation.

To become whole, we need to embrace not only our body, mind, and spirit, but also the different archetypes and ages within ourselves. Honoring what lessons they bring, what wisdom they hold and any wounds that need to be healed.

In older traditions, the classic archetypes included the maiden, the mother, and the crone. And why do we separate woman and crone? Why is it traditionally how we break up different archetypes and identify with them? Are we saying that an 80-year-old woman no longer has a sex drive? No longer has sensuality? Is no longer a woman?

No, when you become a woman that stays with you. So, let's celebrate it every day of our lives, all the way through.

While we're at it, where's the child? Ahh, do you see her peeking around the corner at you? Let's connect with this aspect of yourself. The Child is vital. When we discuss the inner child, we all understand why she's so important.

Think about it. How much creativity is held within the childlike self? When you were a child think of how creative you were. How willing you were to pull out crayons and color. If your parents would've let you color on the wall, I bet you would've. If someone handed you finger paints, you probably would've dove into them even more then you would now, with more pride, more freedom, less expectation, and more wonder. More creative power.

The teenager is also a huge transformation point. When you look at your teenage side this is when we are starting to define yourself. This is when we're starting to step out into the world and test boundaries. This is when we're starting to push back against authority. It's also when we're really starting to demonstrate and formulate who we're going to be in this life. That takes courage. It takes strength. It takes power.

We go through important trials and tribulations that are necessary to mature us. We may feel out of place or become awkward when we grow into our physical form and we start having our first relationships. We experience our first heartaches, our first adventures and our first sexual experiences. Almost all of this happens in adolescence. It's an incredibly transformative time.

This is the initiation period. It's critical for us to honor the teenager within ourselves. It's from there that we become women.

Obviously, womanhood is our opportunity to allow all that to come through. There's a lot of adventure and experience that we step into. There's also a lot of predetermined conventions that we've adopted, which stymies the free exploration of what it means to be a female. Often by the point we embrace womanhood, we've also started to embrace limitations, beliefs, restrictions, and conditions. We may have allowed other people to determine certain styles of living for us.

Perhaps we've been married, had kids, taken on a career that other people said was safe. All of these labels start to formulate and create a framework that we live in. That framework can feel like a tight fit as we continue to grow. It limits how much or how we express our true feminine power, which is not a negative thing. This is something to be aware of when we're embracing all the parts of our feminine side because if we limit ourselves to becoming the woman everyone else thinks we should be, we lose all the gifts we just discussed that come from the child and teenage sides.

Eye opening isn't it?

As soon as I decided to gaze inward and take my child side out, there she was, waiting for me. As soon as I got on my yoga mat, she dropped, and I had to pause my playfulness. I sat back down to write about how I can feel her still smiling at me.

Learning how each of your sides likes to engage with you is key. The child side may want to sing (mine likes to make up songs and belt them gleefully while watching the reactions on people's faces). My teenager likes to think and work. She likes to take projects to completion and feel accomplished. My woman side likes sex, dressing up, and writing.

Today I feel my child side is calling to me – "Come and play with me, come and dance and move your body, I want to feel the air against my skin, I want to play with life, I want to play with being, breathing and simply aliveness." So off I go from the computer to give my little one the attention and love she not only needs but wants.

You can lose yourself by constantly rating how well you measure against that concept of a woman.

But that's a false scale.

It's a scale based not on the actual female energy because, again, the female does not equate to woman. Femininity equates to all the stages in which we're female.

The pressure that can be released by opening up to this wider definition of being a woman is profound.

Because when you stop defining it as this confined version of a woman and start seeing yourself as full featured female, that gives you so much more liberty and freedom. You can define what female energy means for yourself.

Think about it. What's the optimum woman you would strive to be? What's the ideal woman you believe exists?

Let's play another vision game. (If you would like a guided version, remember to use your unique book code to download an audio track from the site.)

Using the techniques, you will have been practicing with the meditation exercises. Stop and take a few deep breaths.

Now, what did you experience?

Mystic Moments

I find myself standing in a swamp, feet sinking deeply into the muddy ground below. I feel my face scrunch up slightly at the mush crushed between my toes. My child side is laughing at the new experience while my teen is somewhat disgusted.

I want to reach down and cleanse the dirt off my arms when I notice a scratch on my hand that must have happened during my journey through the jungle. Where the hell am I? I wonder just as a bright bird flies over head and perches on a branch of a gnarly tree whose roots are reaching down into the mud. All complaints of mud and dirty water leave my thoughts as I stare at the bird. Beautiful, with wings of fire, golden underneath, and spotted blue on his head. A beak that looks lethal, hooked slightly, and eyes the color of night seem to absorb my presence.

I smile, not wanting to startle it, and attempt to begin a stealthier approach, forgetting the swamp I'm caught in. Stumbling forward, I fall straight into the muddy water I'd been hoping to avoid, feeling a sting in my hand where the cut was. Fuck. I think. A shrill laughter pierces the air, at least I think its laughter. My ears are filled with mud and water as I'm trying to push the hair out of my eyes.

Giving up on the struggle, I place my ass straight down in the mud and rest. Following the sound, I look up. The bird is eyeing me. One dark eye tilted toward me. He opens that beautiful deadly beak again and the piercing laugh surrounds me.

This time the sound goes straight to my core, somehow touching my chakras, tickling my root, caressing my sacral, heating my solar plexus, vacuuming my heart, exploding my throat until it reaches my chakra in the back, the bindu, where it stops... and seems to wait.

Full of energy I start to laugh and feel my own pitch rising, and with it, the power of my life force reaching up to complete the cycle of energy.

Through the back of my head, my soul is deeply inhaling the earthen life force, my third eye erupts outward, as if taking a breath and my crown dances its way up past the spirit bird in the trees and up through to the sky seemingly melding with the clouds and beyond.

In this moment, somehow, I realize the comfort of my body, how it's soothed by the cool mud, how the water rushing over it doesn't make it recoil but causes it to sigh in pleasure. My mind had chosen disgust in regard to the swamp, while my body reveled in the closeness to nature.

I saw the divide between body and mind and the need to listen to both.

Why would the bird be my guide? How would I find myself learning to speak the language of my body once again while sitting in a jungle's bed of mud instead of a picturesque place of a beach? I don't know.

Probably because this is where I would be forced to become unpleasantly yet pleasantly aware of its desire and wisdom.

Pulling myself back up with my arms, I wash my legs, belly, and breasts. I rest my head back into coolness and feel a breeze brush against me. I sigh and bring my consciousness inward, not so far as to move past all existence to only the soul, but to bring the soul outward to meet the primal voice of my earthen beauty. My physicality.

I hum and hear my body hum back, joining me. My heart is like a drum creating a beat.

I sway, allowing the mud to spray over me as I raise my arms to send energy out through my fingers and in turn receive the earth's embrace.

I feel the earth goddess stir around me, her smile catching me with a glint of sunlight shining through the branches overhead. Her breath is the air tickling me and I surrender to her seduction. I love her and joyfully receive her embrace.

Why Did I Choose to be a Woman?

What You'll Gain

The Feminine is an amazing energy. One of the questions I've come across repeatedly during classes is, "Why did I decide to be a Woman in this life?" I'm going to challenge you to stop thinking of it that way. Instead think, "Why did I decide to be female?"

If we don't embrace our feminine energy, we're left moving through life waging a continuous war. Discomfort becomes our constant companion simply because we haven't yet accepted a defining aspect of our physical form and a key component to who we are in this life.

When you judge yourself, you're never at peace. Have you considered that those insecurities you often face can be traced back to the simple fact that you're female? Yet, you don't like what that means or perhaps you don't feel that you're doing a good enough job at all the feminine obligations placed upon you.

What has being female meant to you?

As adults we place weight on the connection to our feminine through the reflection of being the ideal woman (whatever that means to us). Here instead of connecting to that ultimate female energy, we're focused on adopting traits that society has scripted for us.

We accept a sort of typecasting.

Belonging to Yourself. This is the essence of being a woman.

How often do you look at yourself and think, "I'm not really a woman..."? In fact, in my classes 95% of the participants say "not yet" as to whether they feel like they are a woman.

We all have a concept, a definition in our head of what "woman" means. We use it to put ourselves down. We feel that we can never measure up. That is based on conditioning, on society, on the media and all kinds of different cultural legacies. But is it valid? No.

If you keep relating femininity to that, you'll never get to the place where you're really feeling the connection.

Feminine now equals female. That's it. You didn't come here to be "a woman" by anyone else's definition. You came to be your own particular representation of the feminine. You chose a female form. Only one stage is what we call woman but it's ultimately female. We're now connecting to that female energy.

Breaking the restrictions of ages and stages, we realize that the child can be full of wisdom and the woman can be full of wonder. Now that we let go of trying to be the ultimate woman, we can focus on being the fullest most powerful female we can be.

What does this do for you? Let's say tomorrow you're at work and you're faced with a problem. You'd like to approach it with creativity and wonder. Unfortunately, when you only come for the adult woman side of yourself, your options are severely limited. Try approaching the problem from your childlike side. You're still in your full-fledged feminine energy, but you're approaching it with the creative childlike mind. This alleviates so much stress.

Later when you need a bit of courage, you're going to push some boundaries, so you pull on your teenage side. Perhaps you need to stand up for yourself with a bit of a cocky attitude. You are a Goddess in that moment through your teenage energy.

The point is that all of these aspects of yourself are equal and hold amazing gifts. It's up to you to call on these different parts of yourself and utilize them. Don't just take time out and play with our inner child, apply her power in life. She's talented, playful, unencumbered, creative and unique. It's so liberating to express ourselves through these different energies. It frees us from comparing ourselves to the definition of a woman that someone else placed upon us.

We need these energies. They're vital in order to become proud of our feminine energy.

Healing the Feminine

Exploring the various parts of our feminine energy is an amazing gift for healing. Just as we hold various feminine energies within us, each one holds different challenges, fears, inhibitions, negative thought patterns, and insecurities within them.

There are many things that have been haunting you and triggering you in life that you haven't been able to heal. This could be because they're locked up from a stage in your life that perhaps you've disconnected from.

As women while we're moving through our daily life, we feel a familiar knot within us. Perhaps something irritates us and we can't understand why.

We will often think, "I don't know why I feel this way, I can't seem to move past it. I've tried meditating, I've tried yoga, I've tried all kinds of stuff and it's just not goingaway."

Can you think of something like that?

Quite often that is because we are not talking to the right aspect of our feminine energy. We're talking to the conscious adult mind.

Let's try an exercise. Think of a challenge that has been haunting you, one that you have put some real effort into overcoming. We're going to go back inwards. To our inner self.

First ask the inner child, why do I feel this way? What's this about?

Then ask the inner teenager, why do I feel this way? What's this about?

Finally ask the adult woman, why do I feel this way? What's this about?

You can even ask your older self for wisdom. Ask her, why do I feel this way? What's this about?

The more we relate and chat with these different aspects of ourselves, the more we're opening and connecting to the feminine energy. Here's an example of one of the discoveries that came up on one of my spiritual retreats.

Anna had been dealing with relationship issues. When she did this exercise and was presented with her child, teen, and woman, the teenager shifted into an older version and stepped forward. Anna asked her, "Why are you still holding on to this relationship that's clearly over?" The teenager responded, "Well, it's because I thought that person would fix me, it would fix all the things that were wrong."

Anna then showed her that she's happy with her life now. Without these energy blocks, life is actually quite good. Showing the teenager all the wonderful things that have happened, and the freedom she's gained from letting this relationship go, allowed the teenager to finally release it.

For the rest of the week, try something – when something triggers you or brings up any negative emotion – stop and ask yourself, "Okay, girls, who's feeling this? Is it the child, the teenager or the woman?"

You'll be able to check in and begin to find the answers. You'll diffuse some of that anger more quickly or at least understand who is triggered so that you can go in, learn how to clear it. It will take you into a much deeper understanding of yourself and allow you to fix the problems that were once a mystery to you.

Blocking Aspects of Feminine Energy

What You'll Gain

Sometimes we block aspects of our feminine energy because of a female who has hurt us. We no longer want anything to do with something that reminds us of them. We never want to be like them.

Think of someone in your life – a relative, family member, good friend, co-worker, nemesis – who has had a negative impact on you. This might be someone who has drained your confidence or held you back. When you're thinking about this individual and the effect she had on you, do you see any aspect of yourself or female traits that you reject because they remind you too much of this person?

Let me give you an example:

Let's say there has been a female in our life who was highly manipulative and controlled people due to her own insecurities. That may often flip something within you and make you say, "I'll never be weak, vulnerable or needy. I'll always be strong."

As a result, you start to reject the softer part of yourself because you know how damaging it is to be manipulated. Subconsciously, you'll move to the opposite end of the spectrum in order to avoid being like that person. Even if the polar-opposite behavior isn't healthy either.

You may not realize it, but you reject an aspect of the feminine, or traits, simply because it consciously or subconsciously reminds you of someone who hurt you.

This is important. – Now, you don't necessarily have to heal your relationship with that person. All you have to do is be aware of the places in which you've blocked that flow of feminine expression because of another woman. You need to heal your relationship with your feminine source. If you block an aspect of the feminine because of someone else, you're blocking it within yourself. Start with your connection to the actual feminine source. To fully receive the power of the feminine, we heal our relationship with it.

Let's break down the process step by step. To get in touch with the blocks to your feminine energy think of the women who have truly impacted you. Who were your major female influences when you were young? Were they positive or negative? You can break them down into two lists. Don't be afraid to look deeply into the scars. How has that changed the way you act and live?

This is where you'll locate your major shifts. Remember, it could be an indirect influence, or it could be someone as close as your mother. You don't have to judge the person or what they did, but instead how it has created limitations within your own life.

Write down everything that comes to mind.

What have you potentially rejected within yourself? Is it a trait, an activity or a passion that you've been repressing because of the influence of someone else? Women who are really out there – powerful, loud and confident – take a stance. We release any grudges against the feminine energy. You're no longer at war inside. You're comfortable with yourself.

Mystic Moments – True Love

She sits and watches me thrash. Witnessing the war I've chosen to wage against the world and myself. She sees me attack over and over again. And she does not interrupt.

She waits until I've exhausted myself. Until I collapse.

Like a swan she approaches me without fear and without condolences but with love. Pure love.

She waits for me to surrender to what happened and to wake up to what is. Right now.

In her embrace I begin to struggle again, not knowing why I must fight. I fight her love even though I crave it. I'm dying for it. But for some reason I fight against receiving it. Her love.

Why?

I wander in the midst of my emotional storm.
Something makes me hunger for this exact moment, to be held in acceptance, and yet I push against her. I want her to fight to hold me.

Why? I ask again.

I realize she is relentless in her embrace, and that I need to fight for myself, just as I am hoping she will fight for me.

I want her to prove my worth and love. Yet I'm underneath it all, wanting to trust myself to receive love from myself and the world I exist in.

I cry, feeling that I've lost. And yet it's this that I needed.
To break, and know love.

To crumble so I can rebuild. I must focus on the rebuilding.

Am I so defined by pain that it has become the source of my
creativity? Could I somehow shift my passion into a center which
does not need to be harmful?

Moving from Manifesting to Receiving

What You'll Gain

I woke up today to a nudge from my inner self. "Wake up," she called, pulling me from between the sheets, forcing me to extract myself from the warmth radiating off of my love drowsing next to me.

"The dance is waiting," she whispers.

I respond, "We were just dancing within our dreams."

She smiles and nudges me again… "Your dreams are but reality in waiting, don't make them hold their breath for you any longer."

So, I took one more look at Armand, climbed out of bed and began the descent down the hall. "Now what?" I asked her. Although my tone may have sounded begrudging, there was excitement within my eyes.

"Now, Breathe," she said. At this point, if I could give a dirty look inward, I would have. I realize it might sound a little insane to have arguments with one's self but, it happens.

I sat down in front of my laptop, curled up in a warm blanket and began my inward journey to uncover the words I would write. Watching my mind dance and twirl, the thoughts of "Why am I not still in bed?!" crept up. Blurs of energy from my inner selves sprinted by and shimmied back, finally standing strong in my mind's eye, gazing back at me. "Good Morning!" she beamed, "Change abounds."

Change has been my constant for the last few years. It has come at me as gentle as a spring breeze brushing back my hair, and as harsh as a thunderstorm crashing down behind me and chasing me forward through the fields. This has taught me two valuable lessons:

1) Never run from change, it will track you down no matter

which country you move to or how thick those covers you're using to cower under.

2) The more you see your life and the world around you with equanimity, the easier it is to step forward and flow with change.

So now I sit quieted down, resting my spirit, taking a breather, and sharing it with you.

After this I'll sit with my inner divine diva and take a few breaths. I'll ask my "selves" which ride is calling us now that the gates have opened. Then I'll breathe deeper and listen.

The Divine I

"Hey, you, beautiful, down there on your knees...

What are you doing?

Who are you talking to?

Why are you kneeling?" Spirit asked.

"I'm praying," replied the woman, eyes meek.

"Ahhh... praying... so you're talking at yourself?" the Spirit asked,
head tilted.

"No, I'm talking to God."

Spirit looked perplexed.

"Are you not a Goddess? Are you not a Creator?"

She looked up at Spirit stunned, stressed, embarrassed.

"No, I'm just a human being."

Spirit nodded as it turned away from her.

"And thus you will stay until your eyes open, and you finally see
what you could be."

The woman got off her knees and followed Spirit.

"I am what I am," she called to it.

"No, you are what you believe," it called back continuing to move away from her.

"Stop," she cried, panic filling her body as Spirit continued to fade quickly.

Colors swirling, Spirit turned and looked at her, waiting.

"I want to be what you want me to be."

Spirit smiled and looked closer at her, "Don't you recognize me?

I am you."

All your life she has been waiting for the moment you'd remember her, you'd remember you.

The concept of Divinity in the self has always been molded by whoever held the cultural reins in any given moment. Although we can trace the roots back to the origins of these ideas in mythology. However, I don't subscribe to any of the traditional ways that would direct how we enjoy holidays like Easter or Christmas. (Okay, I confess, I do love Easter egg hunts which is an old tradition... but that's merely fueling the child in me.)

Instead, I like to see these days of celebration as an opportunity for self-revitalization. Spring has sprung and it's a stunning time to open to a new blossoming of abundance. I invite you to join me and try something simple and unique for yourself. For example, you can see Easter as your own refueling and rebirthing. Don't see it as an opportunity to worship a deity, bow down to a god/goddess or follow a set tradition. Refocus your energy back into your own source and feed the energy you would traditionally send outwards into your physical and spiritual forms.

Part Five Practices – Mistress of Mysticism

Practice 25 – Inner Child Play

Inner Child Connection Exercise – Let's play! Inviting your inner child out to play can calm your nervous system and spark creativity!

1) Think back to your childhood. Was there a safe space you used to enjoy playing in? Feel that space, recall the smells, and the air. Did you go there barefoot, with sock-feet or shoes? Are you indoors or outdoors?

2) When you have your place, tell yourself, you will go and visit it in your upcoming journey.

3) Now lay back and allow your body to begin to sink into the place you're resting, through the ground and into the earth, allowing yourself to fall backwards, knowing you are safe. As you're sliding backwards, you'll see various ledges around you; one will have a green light.

4) When you spot the one with the green light, direct your body towards it. It's a gateway into this memory of this place, within the middle world.

5) If there is a guardian at the gate, greet them and allow them to cleanse you.

6) Thank them.

7) And if you don't, no worries, take a few breaths and then move through.

8) Notice how the air changes. Notice the sounds and the smells. Notice the ground beneath your feet. Are you back in your childhood play space?

9) If yes, take a few more breaths and invite your child side to come out; that's it, just simply call her out, you can use her nickname, or full name or simply your own loving name for her. And when she appears, greet her with warmth and love, and let her know who you are.

10) Now ask her what she likes to do, and what you can do with her to help her have more joy in life.

So, I've taken my inner child outside and there she was waiting for me; as soon as I got on my mat she dropped in, and as I sit back down to write about it, I can feel her still smiling at me.

Practice 26 – Find the Pieces of Your Child Self

The point of this exercise is pure playfulness. Imagine playing hide and seek with your inner child; you're the seeker, finding the pieces of your child self. Enjoy this as it will create a new sense of wholeness and bring you a new sense of courage to replace existing blocks and fears.

You may want to use:
- music (may I suggest something danceable with drums?)
- colorful clothing, accessories, and decorations
- a free space, you can even do this in a park, backyard, living room, wherever you feel free.

Steps:
- Put on your music, allow yourself to begin to move and feel free.
- Picture yourself as a child, not who you are now, or think you were then, but allow the image to form for you freely. Take your time, there's no rush, this is play remember!
- As you move freely, call out to that image, seeking (playfully, lovingly) any pieces of the child who's in hiding for any reason. Don't judge the reason, you don't even need to understand it at this point.
- Picture yourself as a puzzle and allow the pieces that reappear to fit smoothly and simply back into you.
- Wrap up these returning pieces in love. Wrap up your entire self in amazing hot love.
- Love yourself exactly as you are, not who you think you are, should be, or are becoming. But instead, what your eternal radiant soul self is.

Practice 27 – Connecting with Our Child/Teen/Woman

Ready to start working with and getting to know your child/teen/woman sides? Then let's dive in together using the exercise below.

1. Get comfortable and take a few soothing breaths.
2. When you've learned the exercise allow your eyes to close.
3. Remember the Center point within you.
4. Begin to connect deeply to your breathing and allow that breath to carry you to a quiet space within.
5. Allow the breath to soothe your mind and meet different layers of the self.
6. Relax deeper with your breath.
7. Now within your mind's eye, know that you're in a safe space. A quiet space.
8. In this space we're going to invite the child self to step forward. Remember to breathe.
9. Allow your inner child to present herself to you. Witness her. Acknowledge her. Meet her. Love her and allow her to love you back.
10. Notice her age, notice the expression in her eyes. Notice if she's filled with laughter or joy or sadness. Allow her to be whoever she chooses to be as she presents herself to you.
11. When she does, take a moment and let her know that you honor the feminine within her.
12. Allow yourself to truly appreciate this representation of the feminine as a child.
13. When you're ready, take another breath and let's invite in our teenage side.

14. Allow her to enter into your space. Be very open and welcoming, without judgement.
15. Let her know that this is a space without bias.
16. Notice what she's wearing, how she moves. Be open to hear if she has anything she'd like to share with you. Once again honor her for who she is and that courageous feminine energy that flows through her.
17. Finally, take another breath and thank the child and the teenager. Let them know they are loved.
18. Now open up to the woman at whatever age she chooses to appear. Whether she's younger, the same age or older than you are now, allow her to present herself and step forward.
19. Notice her power, her stature. Allow her to express her authentic feminine self. Welcome her.
20. Thank her for being present.
21. As each representation of the feminine presents herself to you, witness a flow of dynamic powerful feminine energy swirling through each one of them.
22. Know that this child, this teen, and this woman reside within You.
23. Create that complete powerful feminine energy within you.
24. Take another breath and ask if any of them have anything they'd like to share with you. Whether it's a feeling, words, or a visual image – allow them to touch you energetically and unleash the flow of that Goddess energy into your system.
25. Allow it to rush into you like a dam that has been unblocked and can finally fully nourish you.
26. Breathe in and allow it to nurture you. Take a breath and when you're ready release it. Thank them.
27. Bring yourself back and open your eyes.

Notice:

Did you struggle with this in any way? Was the Child, the Teen or Woman harder to experience, welcome in or allow to appear? What did they feel like? What did they say?

Notice if any didn't want to come in or resisted at all. Watch for awkward connections.

Was there one that piqued your curiosity that you really want to get to know?

Practice 28 – Letting Go of Another

This is a common but powerful practice for when we have a person or being we need to express something to, and perhaps we can't to them directly or they've passed on. Regardless of the reasons, the chair practice can help you feel like you've spoken your truth. (And I've even seen it positively impact the other person.)

Set up a chair.

Invite in the Spirit of the person you'd like to hear or express your truths to.

Release out – express it. Get vocal, move around, sing, scream – let it out!

And then let the emotions and the person go.

Practice 29 – Pulling on the Feminine to Help with Challenges

Do you have areas of life you're struggling with but are not sure where they are coming from? Aspects of yourself resistant to change, or repetitive patterns? If so, let's tune into your Child/Teen/Woman sides to find out which one may be stopping you from growing (and potentially why and how you can heal it).

1. Let's close our eyes. Take a couple of deep breaths.
2. At the base of your spine, the root of your being, which is the source of your creative power that names us female, I want you to feel the root of you opening up to be filled by the feminine.
3. Allow that wondrous sensual ocean of energy to flow up into you and fill you, to touch different aspects of you that represent the female, to light you up, to make you feel proud, to allow you to feel comfortable being female.
4. Allow yourself to accept yourself as the feminine.
5. As this energy flows in and fills you, notice how it accepts you as you are right now so perfectly. It doesn't judge you, it loves you. The feminine energy appreciates you for existing and for being such a beautiful expression of the feminine.
6. It flows into you.
7. Take a couple of breaths and allow it to pool within your being. As it does, we are going to invite forward the child, that amazing teenager, and that outstanding woman.
8. Allow them to get comfortable.
9. Bring your awareness to this challenge which you may have tried to work through in the past. Bring your

awareness to it and see it form like a bundle of energy. Show this bundle of energy to the child, the teen, and the woman.

10. Ask which one of them is holding this energy. Do any of them hold on to this? Which of them is triggered? Is it one of them who is scared, upset, angry, sad, or agitated? Frustrated? Inhibited?

11. If one of them steps forward, speaks or shows that it is them, thank them. Thank them for showing that they are the ones who have been holding on to this. Ask them, why?

12. Gently listen closely.

13. Let them know you will work with them to release it if they are ready.

14. What can you do to heal this? How can you liberate yourself from it at every level?

15. Take your time, thank them, and let them know you have listened to everything and will be back to work with them.

16. Take another breath and bring yourself back into the room and the current reality in your own time. Allow your eyes to open.

Practice 30 – Preparing For Ritual

Preparation demonstrates your commitment to the ritual. Set aside time to relax beforehand and set up your space. You may also consider:

1) Have an Epsom salt bath and consciously cleanse yourself of negative energy. Feel that you're washing away, not only the day, but also past experiences that no longer serve you. Any fears, subconscious feelings and critical thoughts that hinder your energy flow can be washed away. Don't worry about understanding or labeling them, just let yourself be soothed and relaxed in the bath. When you drain the tub set the intention for the water to release all that stuck energy.

2) Cleanse your ritual space. Burning sage is awesome for this. By smudging the space (smudging means to light the sage and using a feather to brush the smoke around) you clear away any stuck energy in your environment.

3) Cleanse your own energy field by smudging yourself (don't forget the palms of your hands, the soles of your feet and the crown of your head).

4) Some people will also fast before a ritual.

5) Others will do yoga.

6) Ground yourself, using the practice above to ensure your system is centered and confident.

Part Six – Soulphoria

Allow it to slither its way up your spine.

Dance down over your neck, dropping into your heart.

Allow it to embrace you, encompass you, absorb you, rock you until your heat builds to match it.

Then relax into it, breathe, and feel, allow this to be your only focus for the moment, allow it to consume you.

And allow it to take you over the threshold into bliss.

That is Soulphoria.

That is your being breathing through your body.

What You'll Gain

Just like you can't force an orgasm (at least not a true one), you can't force Soulphoria. Get ready to relax into the experience and allow yourself to discover the bliss that is your being, dancing up your spine.

I have had a lasting Soulphoric experience. The kind that tingles through you and remains dancing across your skin like butterfly kisses. Today I realized I found my flow. I'm fully myself without any need to be somewhere or someone else. Content completely in my moment.

Why? How? It was all the work I've done up until this point that led me here. In reality, it was one key area that made all the difference; it was giving myself permission to be just as I am. It's given me the freedom to dance when I want to, to do yoga when requested by my body, to write when my heart stands up and says, "listen," and to flow within my own life rhythm. It feels like an orgasmic epiphany, that moment when your thoughts finally settle, and you embody the knowing that comes from experience.

Today, that was the understanding of what it means to get into and live in the flow. Now my quest will be *how do I stay in it*. I've maintained this state through the day, and I will continue to relax more deeply into it. Not staring at it or studying it, as we do too often when we look too closely at the beautiful things. They get blurry, as we lose focus and perspective. Instead, I'll continue to allow myself to flow as needed and desired, checking in with my body, spirit and mind.

I've realized that I need to let go and not try to control where my energy wants to go, as long as it's in alignment with the body and soul's desires. The shift to the spiritual can often feel like an all or nothing road, but it's not. I've done the bouncing back and forth between the fully spiritual to my contemporary life full of responsibilities, rebounding back and forth.

As I'm coming out the other end of my C Experience, I've realized that spirituality, your own authentic soul-driven exploration of spirituality, is really what's best for you. The spirituality that's aligned to your body, mind and soul. My persona is multidimensional in the true sense. I love adventure and diversity. I love to be logical and academic while also being creative and spiritual. I love it all. So, in order to feed my entire self, I'm learning to be okay with the different aspects, the corporate me and the spiritual me.

To realize I don't have to give one up for the other; I just need to make space and flow with it.

I'm learning to create space, allow the space to exist, breathe deep into the space without filling it. I'm learning to acknowledge when my mind is taking over and I'm being seduced into heavy thoughts. I've learned to say, "No," I don't want that, those aren't mine, and the thoughts leave. I'm learning how to live blissfully within my body with a mind as a spirit.

Today I saw my body as a kingdom, with my spirit/Eternal Self as the king/queen, my body consciousness as my general and my mind as my intuitive advisor. It was the mind side I have to watch to ensure no external voices infiltrate or allow any of my sides to succumb to another's whims. I'm learning to allow my spirit to lead. I'm also learning to listen for the voice of my body and recognize it with the deepest respect and love. I'm learning to trust myself.

I've heard people repeat how they are in love with life in one moment and the next (well perhaps a few months later) they are in tears, pulling at their hair and wishing the affair had never begun.

If you understand the above statement, there's nothing wrong with you. Believe me. I've been there. I'm guessing most of you have felt the inner screams of, "I'm done." The words we use are ironically similar to what we'd say to a lover when attempting to make a break. "I'm finished." "I've had enough."

Every life is a challenge. One moment is a blissful smooth romantic ride across smooth waters, or for us adrenaline junkies, a crazy roller coaster that terrifies us, yet we know we're safe somehow, and yet in the next moment it can change as the dark clouds move in. Thunder strikes a little too close to our physical form, shaking our entire existence. Perhaps it even touches us, kissing us with the force of lightning, igniting our being as it drains us of all energy. Maybe even hope.

I've been there too, staring at my reflection, questioning everything, drained of my lifeblood, or having it stolen by those I cared about most. The question of my worthiness hanging limp in the balance. Events that impugn our self-worth build up like trauma locked in ourselves.

And yet, we must come back to the soul and realign.

Life is a lover we live with every day, one we chose. Learn to either live and move in rhythm with it, or give it up, and walk away from the next breath.

So, what is Soulphoria?

It's that sparkling moment when your body, mind and spirit unite into one, and you're so in the now, that everything else disappears. The unification of the various parts of us allow an energetic highway to unleash your soul energy. It floods every cell of your being, and beyond, to touch the people around you.

In that moment the world around slips away like a silk scarf sliding through your fingers, and you feel your spine straighten as if to say "yes!" to the energy building within you.

You feel the energy pooling at the base of your spine and a slight haze of warm light fills you as you breathe into it. Just when you want to look away you keep focusing inwards, until that energy ignites, joining your conscious thought and your breath. Then it flies upwards, soaring like an eagle up your spine. Wings wide, tickling every inch of you. Then that eagle of light bursts out the top of your head.

To achieve Soulphoria – it takes the ability to let go of the density of the reality surrounding you. It's about tuning inwards and focusing on your soul energy. From there you allow your body, mind and heart to melt into it. Like items of the earth melting into a pool of lava. That melting ignites your energy and embraces you, your entire body, mind and soul.

Mystic women, come to me.

And allow the world within to be.

Your shining place of peace and calm.

Where the fire is fierce and strong.

Allow the oceans of emotion to wane.

And acknowledge your royal reign.

Mystic women, come to me.

And see all your life can be.

Glossary

Binaural Beats – These beats are beautiful but not the typical type you can groove to. These tones can be used to help you relax, learn, and heal.

Channeling – Opening yourself up to the flow of information from your Cosmic Support System.

Comparanoia – When you are constantly comparing yourself to others – Paranoia + Comparison.

Ethereal Realms – Realms where your cosmic support systems exist.

Qi Gong – A practice within traditional Chinese medicine, which combines meditation, movement and breathing.

Author Bio

Alessandra Sagredo is a sought-after spiritual guide and teacher, helping people discover a Soulphoric life. Her writings and teachings make spirituality seductive and tip many of the sacred cows of mainstream spirituality.

Her life has been blessed with numerous beautiful events and challenges as well, including overcoming brain cancer. Alessandra understands that embracing a spiritual practice doesn't mean you are immune from difficulties. Bad things can happen to good people, and one of her goals is to help make you stronger when facing life's challenges. She has been in love with all things mystic since she was a little girl. Although as a child she would often find herself tea-partying with entities, the actual tidal waves of past life recollections began in her 30s and have continued to surprise her to the present day.

Alessandra's formal experience and training include Shamanic studies from teachers such as Sandra Ingerman and Christina Pratt; Qi Gong with Master Mingtong Gu and Dr. Jahnke; and Counseling Hypnotherapy. She is a recording artist for several guided meditations which sold thousands of copies. Alessandra has also been a successful entrepreneur, owning a fabled wellness center in downtown Vancouver, and becoming a sought-after business consultant and public speaker running workshops internationally.

In closing and in her own words

The cosmos has brushed up against me, teasing me into listening.
Flaunting its knowledge like a seductress filled with wisdom.
Knowing. Guiding.
Alessandra Sagredo

Acknowledgements

Thank you to Armand who has taught me what it's like to experience true unconditional love, and who has been there for me cheering me on in the darkest of times. Without you there would be no me to write *Soulphoria*.

Thank you to my Soul Sister, Anjanette Sims, for being there throughout my C Experience and beyond!

Emily Tamayo Maher, who has helped me mold my creative chaos into a beautiful book. She has been my book Doula.

My Ancestors for folding time and space to stand by me during this journey; reminding me I don't have to go at it alone.

My Okanagan Family & Friends for all your support and continued love. To my early supports (beta readers and endorsers!) for your belief in what *Soulphoria* can do for the planet.

And thanks to you, who are reading these words. For being open enough to explore a different perspective of moving through life. And bringing more joy and peace into your life and the planet. Together we can make the Earth a Soulphoric place!

BOOKS

SPIRITUALITY

O is a symbol of the world, of oneness and unity; this eye represents knowledge and insight. We publish titles on general spirituality and living a spiritual life. We aim to inform and help you on your own journey in this life.
If you have enjoyed this book, why not tell other readers by posting a review on your preferred book site?
Recent bestsellers from O-Books are:

Heart of Tantric Sex
Diana Richardson
Revealing Eastern secrets of deep love and intimacy to Western couples.
Paperback: 978-1-90381-637-0 ebook: 978-1-84694-637-0

Crystal Prescriptions
The A-Z guide to over 1,200 symptoms and their healing crystals
Judy Hall
The first in the popular series of eight books, this handy little guide is packed as tight as a pill-bottle with crystal remedies for ailments.
Paperback: 978-1-90504-740-6 ebook: 978-1-84694-629-5

Take Me To Truth
Undoing the Ego
Nouk Sanchez, Tomas Vieira
The best-selling step-by-step book on shedding the Ego, using the teachings of *A Course In Miracles*.
Paperback: 978-1-84694-050-7 ebook: 978-1-84694-654-7

The 7 Myths about Love...Actually!
The Journey from your HEAD to the HEART of your SOUL
Mike George
Smashes all the myths about LOVE.
Paperback: 978-1-84694-288-4 ebook: 978-1-84694-682-0

The Holy Spirit's Interpretation of the New Testament
A Course in Understanding and Acceptance
Regina Dawn Akers
Following on from the strength of *A Course In Miracles*, NTI teaches us how to experience the love and oneness of God.
Paperback: 978-1-84694-085-9 ebook: 978-1-78099-083-5

The Message of A Course In Miracles
A translation of the Text in plain language
Elizabeth A. Cronkhite
A translation of *A Course in Miracles* into plain, everyday language for anyone seeking inner peace. The companion volume, *Practicing A Course In Miracles*, offers practical lessons and mentoring.
Paperback: 978-1-84694-319-5 ebook: 978-1-84694-642-4

Your Simple Path
Find Happiness in every step
Ian Tucker
A guide to helping us reconnect with what is really important in
our lives.
Paperback: 978-1-78279-349-6 ebook: 978-1-78279-348-9

365 Days of Wisdom
Daily Messages To Inspire You Through The Year
Dadi Janki
Daily messages which cool the mind, warm the heart and guide
you along your journey.
Paperback: 978-1-84694-863-3 ebook: 978-1-84694-864-0

Body of Wisdom
Women's Spiritual Power and How it Serves
Hilary Hart
Bringing together the dreams and experiences of women across
the world with today's most visionary spiritual teachers.
Paperback: 978-1-78099-696-7 ebook: 978-1-78099-695-0

Dying to Be Free
From Enforced Secrecy to Near Death to True Transformation
Hannah Robinson
After an unexpected accident and near-death experience, Hannah
Robinson found herself radically transforming her life, while a
remarkable new insight altered her relationship with her father, a
practising Catholic priest.
Paperback: 978-1-78535-254-6 ebook: 978-1-78535-255-3

The Ecology of the Soul
A Manual of Peace, Power and Personal Growth for Real People
in the Real World
Aidan Walker
Balance your own inner Ecology of the Soul to regain your
natural state of peace, power and wellbeing.
Paperback: 978-1-78279-850-7 ebook: 978-1-78279-849-1

Not I, Not other than I
The Life and Teachings of Russel Williams
Steve Taylor, Russel Williams
The miraculous life and inspiring teachings of one of the World's
greatest living Sages.
Paperback: 978-1-78279-729-6 ebook: 978-1-78279-728-9

On the Other Side of Love
A woman's unconventional journey towards wisdom
Muriel Maufroy
When life has lost all meaning, what do you do?
Paperback: 978-1-78535-281-2 ebook: 978-1-78535-282-9

Practicing A Course In Miracles
A translation of the Workbook in plain language, with mentor's
notes
Elizabeth A. Cronkhite
The practical second and third volumes of The Plain-Language
A Course In Miracles.
Paperback: 978-1-84694-403-1 ebook: 978-1-78099-072-9